Trick Photography

Trick Photography

Crazy Things You Can Do With Cameras

By Robert Fischer

M. EVANS AND COMPANY, INC.
New York

Library of Congress Cataloging in Publication Data

Fischer, Robert James.
  Trick photography.

   Bibliography: p.
   Includes index.
   1. Photography, Trick.   I. Title.
TR148.F57   778.8   80-22333

ISBN 0-87131-332-4 HARDCOVER

ISBN 0-87131-335-9 PAPERBOUND

M. Evans and Company, Inc.
216 East 49 Street
New York, New York 10017

Design by Robert Bull

Manufactured in the United States of America

9 8 7 6 5 4 3 2 1

For
Daniel E. Fischer, M.D.
Thanks for being my brother.

CONTENTS

ONE

HOW TO USE THIS BOOK

With trick photography, you can make an ordinary picture extraordinary.

Trick photography allows you to make fog appear where there is no fog and to make spaceships appear to move across a starry sky. You can use tricks to shoot pictures in bright sunlight and make it look like nighttime, and to give someone two or six heads, all without makeup or plastic surgery. Tricks in your prints, slides, or movies can fool an audience, or can let you share with other people the fun of an outrageous shot.

What You'll Need

Most of the tricks in this book can be done with simple, inexpensive cameras. More sophisticated cameras cost more money, and while they may make photographing some tricks easier, they're not necessary for many of the tricks.

How do you know if the camera you're planning to use is simple or sophisticated? Look at the features on the camera itself. If possible, read the owner's manual, which

1

will describe the camera's features. Now check what you've learned against the following explanation of the camera symbols used in this book to see which category your camera falls into.

Camera Symbol Chart

■◻ Simple still camera: A box type camera, or one that takes 110 or 126 size cartridge film. Often has a built-in light meter and can take a flash attachment that uses flash cubes or bulbs. Some 35 mm models may have footage (distance) settings or a rangefinder system for focusing the lens. They may also have *f*-stop settings to adjust the size of the aperture (the lens opening).

◖◻ Sophisticated still camera: Usually 35 mm, with adjustments for focusing through the lens, adjustable *f*-stops that can override the built-in light meter, and adjustable shutter speeds. Settings for different film speeds. May take more than one lens.

Simple 110 camera (on the left) and a more sophisticated, though not that expensive, 35 mm camera (on the right).

Simple Super-8 camera (on the left) and a more sophisticated Super-8 movie camera with through-the-lens viewing and single-framing capability (on the right).

Simple movie camera: Usually silent. Often has automatic light meter; may have hand settings for focus. Can be a low-light camera and may have a zoom lens.

Sophisticated movie camera: Can be silent or sound. Viewing and focusing through the lens. Built-in light meter can be adjusted by hand with a manual override. Zoom lens, often motorized. Single-framing capability. The most sophisticated ones can have fade in, fade out, and dissolve devices, variable motor speeds, and a backwind capability.

Note that each category in this list has a symbol next to it. One or more of these symbols appears at the beginning of each trick. By checking the symbols before you attempt a trick, you'll know if you have the right camera to produce that trick.

In addition to needing a camera, you may find it useful for many tricks to mount the camera on a tripod. This keeps the camera steady, and locks its position. A one-legged stand, called a minipod, may help in some situations.

For use with many still cameras, there is also a long wiry attachment called a cable release, which may prove helpful. This little device screws into the shutter-release button and lets you trip the shutter to take a picture without actually touching the camera. That way there's less chance of jarring the camera out of position.

For single framing animation tricks, first mount your movie camera on a tripod. Then use a device called a remote control switch that lets you advance the movie film a frame at a time without touching—and possibly jiggling—the camera.

Cable releases and remote control switches are fairly inexpensive. A minipod will cost a few dollars more, and a good tripod can be fairly costly. Before considering any purchase, though, first explore the possibility of borrowing the item from your family, friends, or school. If you do want to buy camera equipment, consider buying used equipment at lower prices.

Other Equipment

In addition to such photographic equipment as cameras and tripods, you'll of course need the appropriate film for your purposes, and in some cases perhaps indoor lights.

And some tricks may require more than just a camera and film and light. You might need a mirror, say, or perhaps a filter in front of the lens. Tricks that require even more complicated materials, such as a matte box, a rear screen projector, or toy models (miniatures), are technically classified as special effects tricks.

Peter Ellenshaw, the special effects expert for the movie *The Black Hole,* calls special effects "scenes or events that are not part of our everyday life and cannot be done in a normal way." Special effects often include the use of mechanical or electronic devices and can be very costly. The shark scenes in *Jaws* and the spaceship battle scenes in *Star Wars* are good examples of special effects.

So as not to be too tricky, this book uses the words "trick" and "effect" to mean the same thing. The special effects tricks included here have been selected because they're fun and easy to do. And you won't have to be a millionaire to do them, either. When you do need certain materials, you can find most of them around your home. Items such as window or door screening, cardboard boxes, plastic containers, model toys, or some petroleum jelly, are not too costly and are easy to round up.

There are some tricks that require materials you most likely will have to purchase, such as special mirrors, filters, Mylar, and so on. But such tricks have also been selected with economy in mind. The materials may cost a few dollars, but you will be able to use the items for several different tricks.

Any special materials, whether from around your home or to be purchased, will be listed at the front of each trick. Before plunging into a trick, read over the materials list, much the same way as you would read over the recipe ingredients in a cookbook.

Finding Tricks in This Book

Some of you will want to read this book through from cover to cover. Some of you, though, may want to locate a specific trick right away. To find a trick, check the table of contents in the front of the book. The sections are arranged generally by the kind of material needed to produce the trick. In addition, check the index. This is very important, because often there is more than one way to produce an effect.

Let's say you want to produce a multiple image. You might see the multiple image listing under Rear Screen Projection and Matte Boxes in the table of contents. If you check the index, too, you'll see there are other ways to produce multiple images, such as with a Fresnel filter sheet, or with a mirror. If you check out all the possibilities, you can then decide what would be the best or easiest way for you to make a multiple image.

There are some tricks you won't find in this book, because they're in your own imagination. The section on Combination Tricks in Chapter 9 gives some examples of what you can do when you combine two or more tricks. But you may come up with combinations of your own, depending upon what you need for a particular picture or scene. Feel free to let your imagination run. Part of the fun of trick photography is not just looking at the world in an unusual way, but in finding your own ways to record on film what you imagine.

TWO

THE BASICS

Still and movie cameras work much the way
an eye does. In an eye, light reflected from an
object passes through a lens and is sharply
focused on the back of the eye, the retina, which is sensitive
to light, dark, and color. The information is then carried to
the brain, which interprets what the eye sees. With a camera,
it is a piece of film that is sensitive to light and, if it's color
film, color. Unlike the eye and the brain, cameras don't
interpret what they see; they simply record the information.
And unlike an eye, film is sensitive to only a very limited
range of light, dark, and color.

Still cameras use a roll of film in which each frame is
advanced and held firmly in place as it is exposed to light.
Many film stocks have perforations, or holes, on one or both
edges of the film so the sprockets (gears) can pull the next
frame of film into place. Depending on its length, one roll
will produce 12, 20, 24, or 36 still pictures.

Movie cameras are very similar to still cameras in prin-
ciple. They also use a roll of perforated film in which each

frame is advanced and exposed to light. The major difference between still and movie cameras is that in a movie
camera, the film is advanced at 18 frames every second for
silent Super-8, and 24 frames each second for sound Super-8.
In other words, a movie is simply a series of still pictures
taken in rapid succession.

The movie camera, in order to take so many still pictures each second, must have a strong, but delicate, motor.
A claw pulls each frame of film into place for a fraction of
a second, holds that frame still while it's exposed to light,
then pulls the next frame down into place to be exposed, and
so on. That's what all the clatter is inside some movie
cameras—the motor advancing the film a frame at a time,
but at many frames per second for many seconds in a row.

If movies are just still pictures, why do the pictures
appear to move? A phenomenon called the persistence of
vision explains it. When the human eye sees a picture, and
then another picture, for a split second it remembers the
image of the first picture. When it sees a series of 18 or 24
individual pictures every second, as in a movie, in remembering each image before accepting the next, the eye perceives
the series of still pictures as one continuous moving picture.

What You Need to Know About Photography

You don't really need to know a lot about photography to
produce many of the tricks in this book. If you have even a
simple camera with an automatic exposure meter, you can
start right now and get good results most of the time.

On the other hand, the more you know about photo
basics, the trickier you can get. Why? Because many tricks
are based on bending or breaking the rules of photography.
The result: something out of the ordinary.

To understand the instructions in some of the tricks, it
will be useful for you to be familiar with the concepts of

exposure, focusing, and depth of field. If you are using a simple camera, especially one that has a viewfinder system and does not view the image through the lens itself, you will get better and more consistent results if you are also familiar with the concept of parallax.

Exposure

A picture or movie scene that's not too light or too dark is one that's well exposed. If you get comments on your pictures like "That's too dark to see," or "It's all washed out," you're having exposure problems.

Of course, there may be times when you want a picture very dark. If you want a shot to be suspenseful or mysterious, you may want large areas of shadow. Making a picture lighter than normal may create the desired romantic feel, or if way too light, an unusual or abstract feel. When your pictures are too light or dark and you don't want them to be, though, you're exposing the film incorrectly. Poor exposures can waste film, time, and money, and cause you frustration in not getting the shots you want.

There are three basic ways you can control exposure:

1. *The speed of the film.* Whether color or black and white, still or movie film, all film is sensitive to light to a greater or lesser degree. Slower films are less sensitive to light; faster films are more sensitive to light. ASA and the newer ISO numbers are used to rate how sensitive films are to light. The higher the rating number printed on the film box, the more sensitive that film is to light.

What this means is that in low-light situations, such as in a dimly lit room or when shooting outdoors in the evening, you may need a faster film to make sure you get the proper exposure. And in bright light, such as at the beach or on a ski slope, you most likely will want to choose a slower film to ensure proper exposure.

2. *The shutter speed of the camera.* Super-8 movie cameras rarely have adjustable shutters. Neither do most simple still cameras. So adjusting the shutter speed applies mainly to some simple and to the more sophisticated 35 mm still cameras.

The shutter controls how long the light entering the camera will strike the film. Adjustable shutters measure the amount of time in fractions of a second. Each setting either halves the time the shutter is open, or doubles the time of the previous setting, depending upon whether you're setting the shutter to go faster or slower. A shutter speed of 1/30

The shutter speeds on this still camera are printed on the second round dial from the left. They range from one second to 1/1000 of a second. The *X* by the 1/60 of a second setting indicates this speed should be used for flash pictures. The B setting lets you keep the shutter open as long as you hold the shutter release button down. The settings on the lens are, from the outside toward the camera body, the footage and meter settings, the depth of field scale, and the *f*-stop setting.

of a second is twice as fast as 1/15 of a second, but only half as fast as 1/60 of a second.

If you snap a picture of a moving object at 1/125 of a second or faster, you'll be able to freeze the action. So one advantage of being able to adjust shutter speeds is having the choice to make a sharp or a blurred picture.

3. *The amount of light striking the film.* Cameras control how much light strikes the film by adjusting the opening in the lens, called the aperture. The wider the opening, the more light passes through the lens; the smaller the opening, the less light passes through. Numbers called *f*-stops have been devised to measure the amount of light passing through the lens. Each *f*-stop allows in twice as much light as the one before, or half as much light, depending upon whether you're opening the lens up or closing the lens down. Some cameras allow settings between the standard *f*-stops as well. Look at the illustration to see what size lens opening each *f*-stop makes.

Size of Aperture at Standard F-Stops

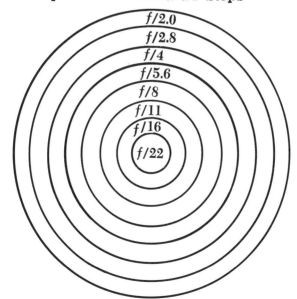

f/2.0
f/2.8
f/4
f/5.6
f/8
f/11
f/16
f/22

Most cameras today come with a built-in light meter that measures the amount of light coming into the camera. Some indicate to the photographer if there's not enough light to shoot. Other cameras automatically open up the lens if there's not enough light; if there's too much light, they stop down the lens. So the cameras are actually setting the *f*-stops for you.

When using still cameras that let you set *f*-stops manually (by hand), how do you know which *f*-stop to use? If the camera has no built-in meter, you'll have to use a light meter, or go by the suggested settings in the brief exposure guide packed with each roll of 35 mm film, or simply guess whether or not there's enough light to shoot and how to set the camera.

Still and movie cameras that allow you to manually override the automatic built-in light meter settings are the most flexible in giving you choices of correct exposures.

How can these three elements—speed of the film, shutter speed, and *f*-stop—help you get just the shot you want? Let's look at an example.

Let's say you're planning to shoot a still picture of someone running outdoors. If you choose a very fast film with an ASA of 400, to get the proper exposure you would have to shoot at *f*/22 at 1/500 of a second. With such a fast shutter

speed, there would be no blurring of the action. (Not all cameras, of course, have such small openings and such fast shutters.) On the other hand, if you chose a very slow film, you'd be at a very slow shutter speed with a very wide lens opening, and the action will necessarily be blurred. Again, you don't have much room for choice.

If, however, you choose a medium-speed film, say one with an ASA of 125, a recommended normal exposure on a sunny day would be $f/11$ at 1/250 of a second. If you want to, though, you could also shoot at $f/16$ at 1/125 of a second, or $f/22$ at 1/60 of a second. Or, going the other way on the scale, $f/8$ at 1/500 of a second. And each of the

You can change the look of a picture by varying the shutter speed and the f-stop. While all these pictures were shot on film of a medium speed (ASA 125), the first shot at $f/2.8$ and 1/250 of a second freezes the action. The second shot is equally well exposed, but the feeling of movement is captured with a blurred runner by shooting at $f/8$ and 1/30 of a second. The third shot has exactly the same exposure as the second, but looks different because the camera was moved in the same direction as the runner. The result leaves the background blurred but the runner, by contrast, sharp and clear.

pictures will come out different, depending upon which combination you choose.

If you want the runner to blur a bit, you'll need to shoot at 1/60 of a second or slower. A shutter speed of 1/125 of a second or faster will freeze the action.

Choosing a shutter speed alone, though, will not create the shot. You have to compensate with the appropriate aperture for correct exposure. In this case if you halve the shutter speed, you need to double the aperture size. Either shot will be correctly exposed, but each shot will look different. Having a choice of combinations for exposure, then, gives you more flexibility as a photographer to get the shots you want.

Here's another example where properly combining the elements of film speed, shutter speed, and *f*-stop will help you. Let's say you're shooting someone who's backlit, either by bright lights or the sun. Remembering that the person's face will actually be in shadow, you choose a fast film to get a good exposure. Now you want to be able to see the person's face, but when you shoot into the light your camera exposes for all the light entering the lens, exposing the sky properly but leaving the face very dark. To get around that problem, you would leave the shutter speed the same but open up the lens two stops. The background will then be overexposed (washed out), but what you wanted was the face and that will come out properly exposed. So in this case, too, manually overriding the *f*-stop will help you control how your picture comes out.

The lens opening is not the only way that you can control the amount of light coming into the camera. Read Chapter 3, Tricks with Lighting, for other ways that you can increase or decrease the amount of light striking the film. This can be particularly helpful when shooting movies, as you may be able to manually override a Super-8 camera's *f*-stop setting, but there will be no way to adjust the camera's shutter speed.

Focusing

When you focus on an object, you make that object appear sharp and clear in your picture. With sophisticated cameras that view through the lens, you can focus precisely on an object. In other words, what you see in focus in the view-finder is pretty much what you get in focus in the photograph.

Simple cameras make everything appear in focus, from a few inches away all the way to infinity, which is as far away as you or your camera can see. (The symbol for infinity is ∞.) Because you are aiming through a viewfinder, and not the lens, though, what you see may not be what you get. While objects close to the camera may look in focus to you in the viewfinder, the lens may read these objects as fuzzy. The result is an out-of-focus picture.

How do you know how close you can get to an object with a simple camera and still keep the object in focus? Some

Six dominoes are out of focus. Multiply by two (because they were set two inches apart with the camera two inches from the first domino), and you have determined that an object must be at least twelve inches away from this camera for its lens to keep the object in focus.

cameras print the number of inches or feet right on the lens, or tell you the distance in the instruction manual.

You can also make your own test shot to see how close your camera can get and hold focus. Set up a series of objects, such as dominoes, diagonally, two inches apart from each other. Set the camera two inches from the first object and snap a picture. When the picture has been developed, count to the first object that is in focus. Multiply the out-of-focus objects by two, and this will give you the distance, in inches, you need to keep your pictures in focus. When you are working with a camera that has *f*-stop settings, you should test separately for each *f*-stop.

Simple cameras that have a rangefinder system for focusing let you turn the lens barrel and match two images until they merge into one. If you look at the lens barrel, you'll see you've selected a footage setting on it that will be fairly accurate.

You can get good results with simple cameras, even if you're not able to view through the lens, by setting distances when possible, or at the very least, by not getting so close to objects that your camera can't hold focus on them.

Depth of Field

When you focus on an object, usually some of what's in front of and also behind the object is also in focus. How much in front of and behind the object remains in focus is called depth of field. Depth of field can be a very useful tool in trick photography, because you can to some extent choose what you want to be in and out of focus in your shots.

A wide-angle lens gives a wider view than the more normal look given by a medium-focal-length lens. A telephoto lens sees a smaller view, but brings it closer.

Depth of field depends mainly on—

1. *Distance from lens to subject.* As you get closer to a subject, the depth of field gets less. As you get farther away, the depth of field increases.

2. *Focal length of the lens.* Focal length, measured in millimeters (mm), is the distance from the optical center of a lens to the point where the light rays converge on the film. A medium-length lens, called a normal lens, sees pretty much what the eye sees. A short lens, called a wide-angle lens, takes in a much wider amount than the eye. And a long lens, called a telephoto, sees much less than the eye, but magnifies the object, much the way binoculars bring faraway objects closer.

What focal length lens is normal, wide angle, or telephoto depends on the size of the film you're using. For 35 mm film, a normal lens is 50 mm, a wide-angle lens is 28 mm, and a telephoto lens is 105 mm or longer. For Super-8 film, a normal lens is 12.5 mm, a wide-angle lens is 8 mm, and a telephoto lens is 18 mm or longer.

Keep in mind that zoom lenses, technically called variable-focal-length lenses, are wide-angle, normal, and telephoto lenses all in one. Depending upon whether you're zoomed out (wide angle) or zoomed in (telephoto) you're actually using a different focal length lens.

What difference does the length of the lens make in terms of what's in focus in your picture? The longer the focal length of the lens, the less depth of field you have. The shorter the focal length of the lens, the greater the depth of field. So a normal or a wide-angle lens will give you greater depth of field than a telephoto lens.

3. *Aperture.* The rule to remember with aperture and depth of field is that the more you stop down the lens, the greater the depth of field. And conversely, the more you open it up, the less the depth of field you have.

Let's put all this together with an example. Let's say you're shooting a model spaceship against a starry background. You want to keep both the model and the stars in focus, because fuzzy stars just don't look real. What can you do to make sure both are in focus—that is, that you have a great enough depth of field?

With a simple camera, because there's only one lens and the automatic light meter will adjust the exposure with-

Choosing the right combination of focal length, *f*-stop, and distance can let you hold depth of field on the model and the stars both. You can also shoot the model with the camera upside down. To see the result, turn this page upside down. The black threads holding up the model are now at the bottom. No one will look for threads coming *down* from the model. The white tubes are straws attached to more strings so the model can appear to move back and forth and across the star background. The star-like background is created by shining lights through pinholes in black posterboard.

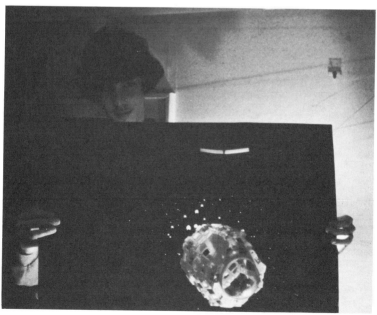

out telling you the *f*-stop, you have only the distance from the lens to the subjects to play with. That means that if you want to fill the picture with the model, you have to make a large model and then stand way back to shoot. Otherwise, if you made a tiny model, you'd have to be right on top of it to shoot, and you may not have enough depth of field to have both it and the stars in focus.

With a more sophisticated camera, you can choose a normal or wide-angle lens, keep the camera far away from the model and the stars, and stop the lens down.

Let's take this example one step further. Because you are going to stop the lens down to hold depth of field, say to *f*/16, this is going to affect the overall exposure. You have to compensate for this small lens opening by selecting the right film speed, and with a still camera, the right shutter speed. In this case, you'd select a fast film and a fairly slow shutter speed so the picture is correctly exposed. With a movie camera, you'd make sure that the lens was stopped down by pumping in lots of light and, if possible, using a low-light camera.

What if you wanted to focus on some object in the foreground while purposely throwing the background out of focus? You'd then select elements that would give you a small depth of field. You'd pick a telephoto lens, move in close to the subject, and open the lens up. But if you've opened the lens up, that will affect the exposure. So to compensate, you'll probably choose a slow film, and with a still camera, a fast shutter speed (or a neutral-density filter) to get correct exposure. With a movie camera, you'd ensure a wide-open aperture by using a slow film and less light.

The knowledge of exposure and depth of field can be very useful in certain situations where not all the elements are variable. For instance, let's say you're shooting something across a busy street, but still want to throw the background out of focus. You can't change the distance of the

The right combination of focal length, distance, and *f*-stop created this picture with very shallow depth of field.

camera to the subject without getting run over. But you may be able to manipulate the length of the lens and the *f*-stop to get a depth of field that will drop off where you want it to.

In tricks, controlling depth of field can definitely help ensure that what you want to be in focus will come out in focus. Follow the rules to create greater or less depth of field. If you want complete accuracy, some photographer's manuals in your library may have depth-of-field charts for different length lenses at different *f*-stops at different distances to a subject. If the distance from the camera to what you're shooting is small enough, use a tape measure or yardstick to make sure you're using the right distance as given on the chart.

For more sophisticated cameras that view through the lens, be aware that many of them let you view with the lens wide open, so the light comes through and it's easier to see. When they film or snap the picture, the lens closes down to the proper *f*-stop. If you want to preview the actual depth of field, use the preview button supplied on some cameras, or manually stop the lens down to the correct *f*-stop. That way you can see exactly what will and will not be in focus when the film is exposed.

Parallax

Through-the-lens viewing systems in sophisticated cameras eliminate the possibility of cutting off people's heads or feet, since what you are seeing through the eyepiece is accurate. With viewfinder systems in simple cameras, though, the image your eye sees through the viewfinder will differ slightly from the image the film records through the camera lens. The difference exists because the viewfinder and the lens are physically in two different places. This difference between what's seen and what's filmed is called parallax, and is a common cause of poorly framed shots that would otherwise have been great pictures.

Parallax Chart

Distance of shot:

$$\underline{5''}$$

$$\underline{4''}$$

$$\underline{3''}$$

$$\underline{2''}$$

$$\underline{1''}$$

$5''\,|\quad 4''\,|\quad 3''\,|\quad 2''\,|\quad 1''\,|\qquad + \qquad |\,1''\quad |\,2''\quad |\,3''\quad |\,4''\quad |\,5''$

$$\overline{1''}$$

$$\overline{2''}$$

$$\overline{3''}$$

$$\overline{4''}$$

$$\overline{5''}$$

With a viewfinder camera, the closer you are to a subject, the more obvious the parallax difference will be. To get well-framed pictures consistently, you have to learn to adjust the aim of your camera to compensate for its particular parallax.

To know just what adjustment to make, you'll need to shoot some pictures. Mark a piece of paper like the Parallax Chart here, except draw the marks exactly an inch apart. Now center the chart in your viewfinder and shoot pictures of it at different distances. Make sure you include in each test photo a piece of paper that has written on it the distance the camera is from the chart.

When the photos come back from the lab, you'll see how far off center your photos actually are at different distances. You can see how many inches too high or low, or to the left or right, the parallax of your camera makes your pictures.

When you shoot your tricks, or even regular photos, you'll know to adjust your camera slightly in the opposite direction, both left or right and up or down, to compensate for the parallax.

When you've seen the results of the first test roll, you can try another, shooting the chart again at different distances. This time, if you know your camera's parallax is to the right and up, aim the camera so the center of the chart is slightly down and to the left in the viewfinder. If you've compensated correctly for parallax, the returned photos will have the center of the chart in the center of the photos.

A Final Word

Even if you've figured out exposure and depth of field as best you can, to make extra certain you'll get the shot you want, you might want to bracket your pictures. Take the shot as you planned it, but also take some pictures at a half stop or a whole stop under and over the planned exposure. You may also want to change the focus or other depth-of-field elements slightly. That way, particularly in an elaborate shot that would be hard to set up again, you've ensured that at least one of the shots will come out exactly as you want it. This can save you a lot of time and frustration in the long run.

Now you're ready to try anything, from putting two halves of different shots together to animating people. Good luck and have lots of fun.

THREE

TRICKS WITH LIGHTING

Some form of light makes all photography possible. The lighting basics presented in the next few pages will help you photograph all your pictures well. The tricks that follow show what happens when you bend a few of the basic lighting rules in your pictures.

Some Basics of Lighting

Outdoor Lighting If the lighting in a photograph is too even, the pictures will look very flat and dull. The more interesting pictures are the ones that have some ratio of light to dark. Black and white film can read as much as a 1:4 (one to four) light-to-dark ratio and still look normal. That means that the dark areas are as much as four times darker than the lit areas. Color film can read areas that are two times as dark as the light areas. This would be a 1:2 (one to two) lighting ratio of light to dark.

Of course, you can also have too high a ratio of light to dark. Sometimes it's necessary when shooting outdoors to fill in shadows, particularly on people's faces. If the sunlight is strong, the shadow area of the face will be more than a 1:2 ratio, and that's more than color film can read. A light meter will measure exactly how much light is striking each side of a person's face. If you don't have a light meter, you'll have to use your eye to judge.

To fill in the shadow areas with some light, you can use white cardboard, or cardboard covered with crumpled aluminum foil, as a reflector. Moving the reflector closer or farther away will achieve the right light-to-dark ratio. Try to position the reflector so that no hot spots fall on the subjects' faces.

You can also use artificial light, such as that of flood-lights or even a flashcube, to fill in shadow areas outdoors. In using that technique, however, you may be mixing out-

A cardboard reflector can make harsh shadows on a face disappear by providing fill light.

door (cool) and indoor (warm) light which may make the color of the person's face in the picture look unnatural. Read the instructions that come with the film you're using to see if you have to filter some of the light to compensate for this difference in color temperature.

Generally, you expose the film for the well-lit side of the face.

Indoor Lighting   Using lights indoors gives you a great deal of control over the look of a picture. Think of indoor lighting as starting from darkness, and you, the artist, are now going to paint with lights, adding them one at a time. Your main light, the one you will use to determine the correct exposure, is called the key light. Just as with the sun, it's

best if the key light is above and in front of your subject and positioned at a 45-degree angle to the side.

Once the key light is set, you may want to fill in the shadows on faces with a fill light. You can use a reflector, a smaller or less intense light, or the same size light as the key light, but placed farther away from the subject. When lights or bulbs are the same size, if you place one light twice as far away from the subject as the other, only one fourth as much light reaches the subject. For black and white film, such a setup would give you a normal-looking 1:4 lighting ratio.

For more sophisticated lighting, you can also add a small light over a subject for top lighting the hair. Consider the amount of top lighting as you did the fill lighting.

The first shot is with a key light only. Notice the dramatic difference between light and shadow. The second shot adds a fill light at a 1:2 ratio, making the face appear less harsh. The third shot adds a top light, also at a 1:2 ratio, for a fully lit picture.

Too Little or Too Much Light What can you do if there's not enough light to shoot as you planned? If you're outdoors and it's getting dark, you have a choice of using faster film, opening up the lens, trying to light up the area, or waiting until the next day. Indoors in low light, you can use a faster film, pump more light in, or place your subjects nearer windows or doorways lit by daylight. Color-compensating filters, or even sheets of gel that cover entire windows, can balance the color temperature if you have to mix indoor and outdoor light.

If there's too much light to shoot, you can use a slower film, close down the lens, or, if possible, cut down the amount of light. Outdoors, you can use shadier areas. Indoors, you can use fewer lights or smaller bulbs, or place the lights farther away from the subjects.

Either outdoors or indoors you can use a neutral-density filter. This smoky gray piece of glass or gel will cut the amount of light striking the film without affecting the color of the picture. These are reasonably priced filters and can help in trick shots that demand a lot of light to obtain an image on film, but in which depth of field must be carefully controlled. To help you figure out the correct exposure when using a neutral-density filter, see the section Using Neutral-Density Filters in Chapter 5.

Ghoulish Lights
a light of some kind
sheets of colored plastic (optional)

Want your ghouls, goblins, or other grotesque characters to look particularly grotesque? Shine a light (even a flashlight) from off camera onto the character's face from below. Try colored materials, especially green, over the lights for even more ghastly effects. (Be careful to use heavy plastic, not cellophane, and to keep materials away from the heat of

Bottom lighting creates a ghoulish effect.

the lights to avoid any danger of fire.) The shadows that bottom lighting creates are positively evil, and are guaranteed to help sicken audiences with even the strongest of stomachs.

The Shadow Knows

Instead of showing the bad guy right away, let his shadow creep into the picture first.

Shadow boxing, anyone? If you shoot early in the morning or late in the evening, shadows become long, pointy, and sometimes very funny.

How about a no-cost crash? If you want to crash two friends, bikes, or vehicles together, show them approaching one another in one shot. In the next shot, show the shadows of the objects coming together. You can simply overlap the objects, but the shadows will make them look like they've

Shadows can add mystery or comedy to your shots.

hit head on. Then have a third shot of your friends on the ground, or the fallen bikes. To make the scene even more realistic, add some crash sounds on your sound track.

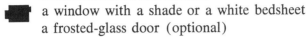 **Silhouettes in the Shade**

a window with a shade or a white bedsheet
a frosted-glass door (optional)

Want to show something horrible without messing up your carpets? Instead of showing the villain committing the crime, show him and the victim in a window shade. Shoot in the evening outside a window with a pull shade. Light your characters with floodlights behind them, pointing toward the window. You'll see their silhouettes on the shade.

Don't have a window handy? A white bedsheet and the same kind of strong backlighting will produce the same silhouette effect.

Use silhouettes to stage a bloodless fight or a kissless love scene.

Silhouettes also work well if you have a love scene and two friends who would rather die than kiss. You can position the two actors so that their silhouettes appear to be touching lips, rather than having them do the real thing.

A frosted-glass door in an office will create an interestingly distorted silhouette if someone behind the door is correctly lit from behind. Even two people talking with the sun behind them can be a striking, dramatic way to fake a dialogue scene. Instead of opening the lens up so the audience sees the faces, expose for the sun and let the faces go dark. You can add the words later without worrying about matching the words to lip movements, because the audience won't see the lips move. If you really want the audience to concentrate on the words, use this kind of backlighting silhouette where the characters have to whisper. You'll have your audience leaning forward on the edge of their chairs, trying to catch every word.

 Turning Lights into Streamers
tripod
fast film
cable release (optional)
zoom lens (optional)

Sometimes photographers create trick photos just for their beauty—the flow of form or color or pattern that pleases the eye. Turning something as simple as car headlights and taillights into beautiful streamers is such a trick.

Set the camera on a tripod, and use a cable release if possible. Pick a spot at night that will place you above or over cars in the street. A bridge, an overpass, a balcony, or even a second-story window may all be good spots.

Use fast film and set the camera on a long (1 or 2 second) exposure as cars streak past. If possible, experiment with longer exposures if you have a T or B setting on your

Using long exposures on moving lights can create beautiful patterns and images.

camera. A B setting allows you to hold the shutter open with one push of the shutter button, closing the shutter when you release the button. A T setting lets you open the shutter with one push, and close it with a second push. Try exposures of 5, 8, and 10 seconds to see what they'll look like.

You can also get the streamer effect by moving the camera itself, using equally long exposures, and pointing at, say, streetlights, or even a brightly lit moon. Get a friend to drive you at night and try a half- to full-minute exposure of lights out the car window for a really colorful shot.

A variation of these streamer shots is to set the camera lens so the lights are out of focus. The streamers will cut wide, wormlike paths across your photographs.

Another trick, with a zoom lens, is to set the camera for several seconds and zoom in or out on some lights. The result will make still lights appear to have streaked across your picture.

Instead of moving the lights, use a zoom lens and a long exposure to create streamers.

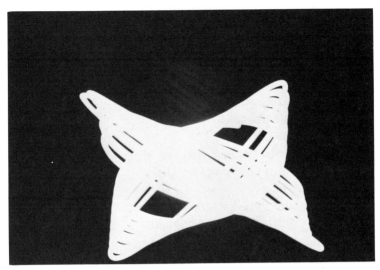

This penlight pattern used two swings of the penlight. With color film, you can add gels over the lens to make colorful geometric patterns.

 Penlight Patterns
string
a penlight
medium-speed film
colored gels (optional)

To create geometric patterns, suspend a penlight by a string, at least 30 inches above the area of the picture. Just holding the string with your hand is fine since it will be in the dark. Set the camera for the correct distance, and use an $f/5.6$ aperture and a medium-speed film. Place the camera on the floor pointing up at the penlight. Turn off all the room lights, set the camera to the B setting, open the shutter with the cable release, turn on the penlight, and let it swing in the air for about 20 seconds.

If you want to add more than one set of patterns to the same shot without double exposing, simply put the lens cap over the lens while you push the light in a different direction or change the length of the cord. You can even add different colored gels over the lens.

When you feel you've gotten the pattern or patterns you want, release the shutter to end the shot.

■ Light-Sword Fights, and Other Things That Glow in the Dark

> two short broom handles (or wooden dowels)
> two long broom handles (or wooden dowels)
> reflective tape or ribbon
> a high-intensity light
> gauze or a fog filter (optional)
> household bleach or rubbing alcohol (optional)
> small brush (optional)

If you want to create a light-sword fight like the one in *Star Wars*, here's an easy way to do it. Have your actors hold the short pieces of broom handles (or wooden dowels). When you want the swords to appear, tell the actors to "freeze." While the actors hold still, stop filming. Have someone exchange the short pieces of broom handles for longer pieces on which you've taped reflective tape or ribbon (available from hardware or fabric stores). Shine a floodlight or high-intensity light from as near the camera as possible directly at the reflective tape. (The lamp should be on from the start of filming.) Start filming again and have your actors proceed with their fight.

If you want the swords to glow even more, shoot through one or more layers of gauze or, if you have one, a light fog filter. The whole scene will become a little hazy, but the swords will appear to glow. You can also take the film after it's been developed, and with a small brush dipped in house-

Glowing light swords appear miraculously out of broom handles.

hold bleach or rubbing alcohol, carefully trace over each frame on the emulsion (dull) side of the film where you want the swords to glow. You can use this in addition to the gauze, or if you don't want the whole scene hazy, instead of the gauze.

You can also use pieces of reflective tape (called "Scotch-lite") or ribbon, with strong light shining directly on it, for lit-up windows in your spaceship or house models. Often this method is easier and safer than trying to rig lights, and your results will be, well, just glowing.

FOUR
TRICKS WITH LENSES

Lenses are the optical means by which you capture images. For a detailed explanation of how lenses work, see the section in The Basics.

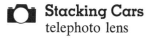 **Stacking Cars**
telephoto lens

You can make cars appear to be stacked up in a pile without going to a junkyard or hiring a crane. Use a telephoto lens on a still camera and photograph a stream of cars on a highway or busy street preferably from a low bridge or overpass. The long lens will appear to compress the cars, making them appear stacked one on top of another.

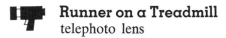 **Runner on a Treadmill**
telephoto lens

With a movie camera, a telephoto lens can make a runner's jog seem endless. Have the runner head directly toward the

Using a long lens makes objects appear compressed, like these cars that look stacked one on top of another.

camera. As the runner gets closer, you'll have to adjust the focus so he stays clear. A long telephoto lens will tend to make even a short run at the camera seem like the runner is on a treadmill and barely getting closer at all.

 The Appearance of Motion
zoom lens
tripod

One way to give the feeling of motion to a still picture is to shoot a subject with a zoom lens. Choose a slow shutter speed and place the camera on a tripod. As you snap the picture, zoom in or out a little bit. The center of the shot

A zoom lens on a still camera can produce this action blur, giving the appearance of motion in a still shot.

will remain in fairly good focus, but the edges of the picture will be filled with an action-packed blur.

In a subject that's moving, you can create a feeling of motion with even a normal lens by choosing a slow shutter speed. The background will remain clear, but the subject will blur slightly. If you want to blur the background, move the camera sideways (called panning) with the moving subject. The subject will stay sharper than the background. To get the maximum feeling of movement, have the subject move sideways rather than toward or away from you.

About Close-up Attachments

Bugs and crawly things can make great monsters in your movies or still pictures, but many cameras can't get close enough to keep the image in focus.

Close-up attachments that fit over your camera lens can bring the little fellows into focus, without requiring additional exposure changes. One of those attachments, called diopters, comes in various strengths, which are called +1, +2, +3 all the way up to +10. You can combine diopters, if you like, placing the strongest one (the higher the number, the stronger the lens) closest to the camera lens. Check with your photo store to make sure you get the right size diopters, and to see if you need a diopter ring to attach the lenses to your camera. The lenses will come with instructions telling you how big a field your camera will actually be viewing, and how close to the subject you will be able to maintain focus. They will also explain in detail that the smaller aperture settings should be used to maintain high-quality photographs.

Some tips on using diopter lenses: Insects can move rather quickly, so be prepared to shoot fast. Because you are magnifying the objects, even small shadows may take up a large part of your picture. Use a piece of white cardboard or foil to act as a reflector to fill in deep shadows. If you're shooting indoors, light that is too bright can wilt plants or kill insects, so take care to use it sparingly and to shoot quickly.

Besides the diopter lenses there are also macro lenses for close-up shots. Some movie cameras now come with macro lenses built in. Macro lenses for still cameras are generally quite expensive, but your school may have one. Diopter lenses and macro lenses do essentially the same thing, that is, bring objects closer to view, but the macro lenses are more costly, and you will lose as much as two aperture settings. Macro lenses are very helpful for shooting movie titles and stills of such objects as stamps and coins.

These stamps were shot with a macro lens, which allows you to shoot close up without losing focus or distorting the shape of the objects.

You may be able to attach some cameras to binoculars, telescopes, and microscopes with special devices. Check with your photo dealer. Using these optical instruments can bring anything from the stars to microbes within the realm of your photos, and ultimately, the tricks you do.

Because telephoto lenses are expensive, you might want to look into using the much less expensive teleconverter. This device fits between a normal lens and the camera body. A 2X teleconverter would turn a 50 mm lens into a 100 mm lens. You will lose a couple of stops in exposure, and the edges may go a little soft, but that might actually be desirable, say, for instance, in portrait work.

▄▆ Fading In and Out

Fading out one image and fading in another usually means a passage of time or place has taken place in your movie. Some sophisticated cameras have built-in fade devices. You can make your own fades, though, if your movie camera has a manual override for the automatic exposure system.

To fade in, first determine the correct exposure with the automatic meter. Now start filming the scene with the lens closed down and gradually open up the lens to the proper *f*-stop for correct exposure. A one-, two-, or three-second fade will be plenty. On screen a longer fade will seem far too long.

To fade out, start with the correct exposure and gradually close the lens down using the manual override.

A variation of the fade to or from darkness is the fade to or from white. Outdoors, to fade in from white, determine the correct exposure. Now start filming with the lens wide open (very overexposed). Gradually close the lens down to the proper exposure.

To fade out to white, start with the correct exposure, then open up the lens till the film overexposes to white.

If your camera has no manual override, but does have a focus control, you might try a trick similar to a fade. To make a fake fade-out, rack the scene quickly out of focus. To make a fake fade-in, start completely out of focus and bring the scene into sharpness. The feeling is not quite the same as a fade-in or fade-out, but your audience will get the idea of a change of place or time.

FIVE

TRICKS WITH FILTERS AND THINGS THAT ACT AS FILTERS

A filter is a piece of material that lets most of the light that strikes it pass through but that removes or distorts or in some way changes some of that light. The result is a special look to the photo or scene filmed.

You can use objects in your home to create your own filters. You can also buy glass filters that screw onto the front of a camera lens, or gelatin filters that can be mounted on cardboard slide frames and placed in front of a lens.

Because filters allow less light through, to get a correct exposure, you have to compensate by opening up the lens. A camera with a built-in light meter will do this automatically. If you use a separate reflective light meter, simply hold the filter in front of the meter to get the correct f-stop reading. With still cameras that have adjustable f-stops and shutter speeds, you can adjust the shutter speed instead of the f-stop, or use a combination of both f-stop and shutter-speed adjustments to compensate for filter and get a correct exposure.

Whether you're trying to create fog on a cloudless day, rainbows when there's no rainstorm, or a starry sky in broad daylight, filters may just fill the bill.

▣ Color Me ...
colored plastic or glass
colored filters
polarizing filter

Want to make your outer-space set red like Mars? Shoot through a piece of red plastic or cellophane.

Any colored plastic material can work as a filter. In cameras with viewfinders, make sure you cover the lens (as well as the viewfinder, if possible) with the material.

Your main character in a blue funk? Shoot him through a piece of blue plastic.

Want to make your audience seasick? Shoot through green plastic.

When you shoot color film, placing glass or plastic of a certain color in front of the lens will turn the whole scene that color.

If you want just part of a scene to turn a certain color, try placing colored plastic or glass in front of a light and aiming the light on the object you want colored. CAUTION: Do not place cellophane near lights as it may cause a fire. Keep plastic and glass at a distance from the light, too, so they do not become too hot.

With black and white film, colored filters have a different effect. A colored filter will lighten objects its own color, and darken objects of its opposite color. A green filter will make leaves on trees look lighter. A red or orange filter will darken blue skies, which can look very dramatic if you have big fluffy clouds. Darken the sky enough, and you can make it look like a storm is brewing. Refer to the Color-Opposites Chart here to select the right color filter for achieving the effect you want on black and white film.

Color Chart

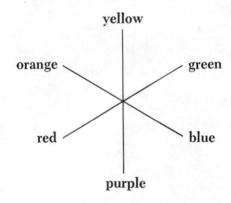

The first shot of the trees is without a filter. The second shows the dramatic darkening of the sky by using an orange filter with black and white film.

If you want to darken a sky with color film, but don't want to turn the whole scene blue, use a polarizing filter. With the sun off to your right or left, as you turn the filter the sky will darken without affecting the other colors in the picture.

 Day for Night
a dark blue filter and daylight film
or
tungsten (indoor) film
or
a deep red filter and black and white film

Day for night means shooting during the daylight a scene that's supposed to look like nighttime. The main lighting source at night is the moon, which is simply reflected sunlight, but which may not provide enough light to show what's going on in a scene. Some night scenes can now be shot with fast film and lights, but day for night allows shooting large areas which are hard to light, such as a lake.

Day for night doesn't look like real nighttime, but film audiences have come to accept day-for-night shots as meaning nighttime, just as they accept a dissolve as meaning a change of place or time. There's a special Hollywood look to day-for-night shots which you may want to capture in your shooting.

Hollywood filmmakers often shoot day for night because film crews have to be paid more for shooting at night. You may find shooting day for night not only solves some lighting problems, but may be more convenient and practical than shooting at night.

Filters and underexposure are the key ingredients in day-for-night shooting. Automatic-exposure cameras will compensate for filters, but you *don't* want that in this case. You'll need to manually override the automatic-exposure setting so that you can underexpose the film one and a half to two stops. With cameras that don't have automatic exposure, set the lens markings for underexposure.

For daylight-balanced color film, use a dark blue filter and expose as though the filter weren't there. For indoor-balanced (tungsten) film, simply *don't* use the 85 filter (often built in to the camera), and underexpose (close down) up to two stops at the tungsten film speed. For black and white film, use a deep red filter and expose as though you were using no filter.

Here are some tips that will make your day-for-night shots even more realistic, so the audience will get more of the feel of nighttime.

1. *Avoid shooting the sky.* If you can, get up high and shoot down. If you must have sky in the shot, use a Pola-filter to darken the sky. You can also use a graduated neutral-density filter. Such a filter will be half neutral-density and half clear, with a gradual change from neutral density at the edges to clear in the middle. Use the dark neutral-density half for the sky to make it look darker. Remember, though, that you can't pan or tilt (pan up and down) with this filter, which is one of the "split" filters. ND filters are discussed further later in this chapter.

2. *Try to include shadows.* Use the sun to backlight or sidelight your subjects. Avoid front lighting.

3. *Put lights in the shot.* Headlights, flashlights pointed at the camera, building lights, sunlight reflected on a lake, Coleman lanterns, and streetlights will all help to give the scene a nighttime feel. If you're shooting in broad day-light, some of these lights may not show up well. You can cheat some lighting by replacing normal bulbs with stronger ones, a lamp bulb, for instance, with a photoflood.

A time to shoot spectacular day-for-night shots is just before sunset. Lights show up better, and campfires will look bright and fiery, not washed out. Your audience will get a strong feeling of nighttime, yet there will still be enough daylight to see expressions on faces. The magic hour is short, so plan ahead and rehearse your shots in advance.

Knowing how to shoot day for night allows you to choose whether to shoot a trick that most audiences readily accept, or to shoot the real thing. Let what you're trying to say or show in a night shot, together with practical considerations, help you decide which option to choose.

A Foggy Day
piece of lens-cleaning tissue for cameras
telephoto lens (optional)
Vaseline
piece of glass

Fog can add a mysterious or moody look to a shot. It's a rare occasion, though, that fog happens to be around when you need it. You can create instant fog by shooting through a piece of lens-cleaning tissue. Use a telephoto lens if you want to make the fog seem a little finer.

If you want a foggy effect on only part of a shot, try smearing a ring of Vaseline lightly in one direction on a piece of clear glass. You can buy inexpensive framed glass at drug, art, and stationery stores. If you smear the Vaseline toward the edges of the glass, leaving the center clear, when you hold the glass up in front of the camera lens, the outer edges of the photo will appear to dissolve into a mist. The center, where your action is, will appear normal.

Rain and Snow
a garden hose or a household sprayer
a polarizing filter
flake soap powder
an electric fan (optional)

A lens-cleaning tissue turns this model town's bright day into a moody, overcast, misty one.

To put rain in your films on a sunny day, a garden hose off to the side of the action and out of frame can provide a good shower. To darken the sky a bit, use filters as described under Making Reflections Appear and Disappear: The Polafilter, in this chapter. For models, use a household sprayer filled with water. Just a spritz or two will make showers appear to fall on your model cars or whole village.

You can add snow to your model scenes by using a flake soap powder such as Ivory Snow. Let a handful trickle through your fingers to make a winter wonderland. If you want a storm to build up, use a fan to blow the flakes into drifts. (Shooting in slow motion helps this effect.)

Distortion and Abstractions

a drinking glass

or

an ashtray

or

a piece of textured glass or plastic

or

a filled fish tank

Your main character has just (*a*) been bopped on the head, (*b*) come out of a deep sleep, or (*c*) been slipped a Mickey Finn drink. Shoot the next shot through textured glass or a plastic object from around the house and your audience will feel just as woozy as your character feels.

You can leave the exposure alone most of the time when you shoot through a drinking glass, an ashtray, textured glass such as a shower door, or even a fish tank filled with water. Experiment a bit with how far away to place the glass or plastic object from the camera lens. Changing distances will often change the look of the effect. Moving the "filter" while shooting may make the effect even more abstract and distorted.

Shoot through textured plastic, such as this tissue box,
to create distortions.

Turn this picture one quarter turn to the left, and the eye
seen through a crystal ashtray takes on an even more
abstract look.

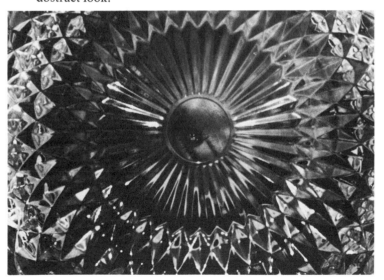

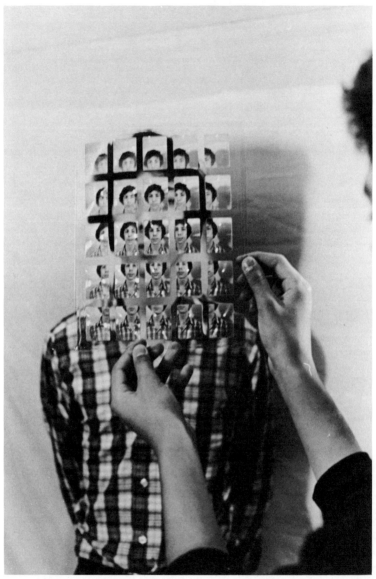

Twenty-five heads can sometimes be better than one. Use a
Fresnel plastic sheet to produce the multiple images.

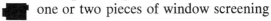 Multiple Images
a Fresnel 25 lens sheet
or
a multiple-image filter

You can create an army out of one toy soldier, or show the fear in a character by multiplying the image that scares him. Shoot through a Fresnel 25 lens sheet (available from Edmund Scientific Company, Edscorp Bldg., Barrington, N.J. 08007) to create as many as 25 images of the same object or person. This method is also very inexpensive. Vary the distance of the Fresnel sheet from the lens to get the size and number of images you want.

For more predictable results time after time, you can buy, at greater cost, a multiple-image filter that will repeat an image three, four, five or more times. With movies, try moving the filter or Fresnel sheet while filming to add an abstract or distorted feeling to the scene.

Starry, Starry Night—and Day!
one or two pieces of window screening
or
a cross-screen filter
clear plastic wrap

When you want to accentuate the lights in a night photograph, you can shoot through a piece of door or window screening to create flares that look like sparkling stars around the lights. Shoot through two screens held at an angle to each other to create even more points on the stars. If you want, you can also buy a cross-screen filter that will create this same effect.

To get a sparkly look, shoot through clear plastic wrap that you've wrinkled and stretched back out. Shine a light on the front of the wrap to bring out the sparkles even more.

These chandeliers were shot through a cross-screen filter, adding points to the lights.

Clear plastic wrap gives this set of braces an extra sparkle.

A Fire That Doesn't Burn
clear plastic wrap
orange filter material
electric light
color film

You can create the look of fire without ever using a match or burning down your model sets. Choose a model with an open window or doorway. Place clear plastic wrap behind the opening. Put orange colored glass or plastic filter material in front of a light that you shine on the plastic wrap. Have someone move the plastic around, or use a small fan to make the plastic flap in the breeze. When you shoot the scene in color, it will look like fire is leaping out the window or doorway.

CAUTION: Do not use orange cellophane near the light, as it may cause a fire. Keep the glass or plastic orange filter far enough away from the light so that it does not overheat.

Using Neutral-Density Filters

You're shooting a picture where you need a lot of light so you can have a small aperture and great depth of field. You've chosen a fast film and a strong light source, and, oops, now you have too much light. You need an *f*-stop of *f*/64, which you don't have, or you'll overexpose the film. One simple solution: Use a neutral-density filter.

Neutral-density filters are smoky gray glass or gelatin that fit in front of a lens. ND filter material also comes in larger sizes that fit over light sources such as flash attachments and even sheets to cover whole windows and doorways. ND filters cut out light without affecting the color of a shot, and come in different strengths. An ND #3 effects a light reduction of one *f*-stop; an ND #6, two *f*-stops reduction; and an ND #9, three *f*-stops light reduction. You

can combine ND filters, too, so using an ND #3 with an
ND #6 will equal an ND #9, or three *f*-stops in light
reduction.

Using an ND #3 on the situation described at the beginning of this section would reduce the *f*-stop to *f*/32; an
ND #6 would reduce the *f*-stop to *f*/22; and an ND #9
would bring the *f*-stop down to *f*/16, which most cameras
can handle. So in certain tricky lighting situations, a neutral-
density filter can enable you to get the correct exposure,
quickly and easily saving an otherwise ruined shot.

Making Reflections Appear and Disappear: The Polafilter

Your main character has lost a precious object. He looks in
a puddle of water, but sees only his own reflection. Then
he looks harder, and as he sees the object at the bottom of
the puddle, his reflection disappears, and we, the audience,
see the same object. Magic? No, just a clever use of a
polarizing filter.

The gray glass Polafilter that fits in front of a camera
lens rotates to reduce or intensify reflections off the surface
of water or glass. You have to experiment, turning the Polafilter to see in what position the reflections are the most
intense and in what position they are completely eliminated.
A Polafilter does not usually affect the color of a scene,
though if the sun is off to your right or left, a Polafilter
can darken a blue sky.

When you want to reduce glare, a Polafilter can help
you get that important still shot of a museum piece behind a
glass case. It can help you shoot through store windows
without seeing distracting or unwanted street traffic reflected
in the glass.

For films, not only can you have characters and audiences
see objects, you can make characters seem to appear or

Turning the Polafilter in front of the lens will increase, reduce, or eliminate glare.

Now you see it, now you don't. While the boy's shadow remains, his reflection disappears by turning the Polafilter.

disappear by shooting their reflections off glass or water and then rotating a Polafilter in front of the camera lens. You can make objects or people appear or disappear in windows, which is great if you have a character who thinks he's seeing things or is being followed.

Automatic-exposure cameras will adjust for any changes in exposure as you turn the filter. Manual cameras should be opened up an average of one and a half stops for correct exposure. Depending on the Polafilter's position as you rotate it, though, you may need to open up as much as two and a half stops.

If you combine two polarizing filters, you can use them as a variable neutral-density filter. As you rotate the two polarizing filters in opposite directions, you reduce the amount of light let into the lens. If you go from one extreme to the other, you can use two polarizing filters as a device for fading in or out. The picture will appear to go from no light to correct exposure, or vice versa, as you rotate the filters. You'll have to practice positioning the filters before you actually shoot.

SIX

TRICKS WITH MIRRORS

A classic way to add suspense to your movies is to have your character rummaging around a room with a simple mirror in it. The audience knows the villain is somewhere nearby. Suddenly, the bad guy's image pops up in the mirror. The audience sees him before the character does. Want to skip the suspense and just scare the daylights out of your audience? Have the character and the audience see the killer's or monster's grisly face reflected in the mirror at the same time.

Mirrors can also make houses look flooded, create two-headed or six-headed people, put a ghost in your film, or wipe one filmed scene away with another.

Any surface that reflects can act as a mirror. You can make interesting and unusual shots photographing reflections off glass; a house, store, or car window; a vending machine; chrome on a car; or even the front of a TV set.

Traditional mirrors found around the house are glass with the back surface coated with silver or some other substance that reflects. When you place the tip of a pencil right

65

to such a back-surfaced mirror, the pencil tip's reflection is not right on the surface of the glass, but the distance of the thickness of the glass away. If you use back-surfaced mirrors to do the tricks in this chapter, you may get some double images (also called ghost images), because the camera will see reflected images on both the silvery surface and the surface of the glass.

To avoid double images when you don't want them, you can use what are called front-surfaced mirrors. These have the silvery coating on top of the glass. They're available in a number of sizes fairly inexpensively from the Edmund Scientific Company, Edscorp Bldg., Barrington, N.J. 08007. When you hold a pencil tip to a front-surfaced mirror, the reflected tip and the real tip touch. There is no space between the images, so no double image forms.

This poor lion doesn't know whether it's coming or going. Neither will your audience.

Whether you're using real mirrors or some other surface that is acting as a mirror, focusing can sometimes be a problem. Do you focus on the surface of the mirror or at the distance the object seems to be behind the mirror? The answer is, the longer distance: You focus as if the subject were as far away as it looks.

If you have a camera that focuses through the lens, you can see through the eyepiece how to keep your subject in focus, letting the rest of the picture go fuzzy. If you can't focus through the lens, measure the distance from the film (not the lens) to the mirror and add the distance from the mirror to the subject you want in focus. That will give you the correct footage setting.

You can often control the amount of reflection off a surface—eliminate it, reduce it, or intensify it—by using a polarizing filter for the desired effect. See the previous chapter for more information on the Polafilter.

◼◻ Which Way Did He Go?
a toy animal, train, or car
a mirror

Set up some object, a toy animal, train, or car, say, to photograph. Then set up a mirror vertically between the camera and toy. The toy will now look as if it doesn't know whether it's coming or going.

◼◻ Shooting Round the Corner
a mirror

Want to take some sneaky peeks? Set a mirror at right angles to what you want to shoot and stand out of sight. You can take pictures—from above, from below, or from the side—without being seen.

⬛⬜ Distortions with Mylar
⬛   a sheet of Mylar
    fast film

You can use plate glass windows of office buildings to give you distorted reflections. Or for really weird distortions, use Mylar.

Silver or chrome Mylar is a petroleum product available in plastics supply stores. This thin material costs about one dollar per foot and comes off a roll about four feet wide.

If you don't want permanent fingerprint smears on the Mylar, handle it by the corners or with soft cotton gloves. Avoid folding the Mylar, as it also creases easily and permanently.

Focusing can sometimes be difficult with Mylar, and parts of some images may simply remain out of focus due to the nature of the Mylar. Use fast film, so you can keep a small aperture and a fair amount of depth of field.

Indoors Lay the Mylar down on carpeting. The hills and valleys help create some distortions. If you want to distort more, place objects underneath the Mylar. When you see the picture you want, snap fast. Mylar and its reflections shift easily, and you may never see quite the same picture again.

If you use lights or flash, point them at the people or objects you're filming, not the Mylar. Choose a distance that will allow you to use an *f*-stop of *f*/16 or smaller. With a flash, the distance from the flash to the subject, not the Mylar, determines the *f*-stop. You may want to open up the lens half a stop.

Outdoors It's best to place the Mylar under a tree or in some other shady spot. Avoid having direct sunlight strike the Mylar as the reflections can be too bright to look at.

Mylar creates weird distortions and abstractions. No two shots are ever alike.

And even a gentle breeze will change the image you see in the Mylar, so again be prepared to snap quickly. Since Mylar may give you false light meter readings, bracket shots at half and whole stops above and below the meter reading to ensure at least one correct exposure.

For scenes where you want distorted lighting, bounce your lights off the Mylar sheets. The results will be unpredictable and weird.

If you can't find Mylar, try using the reflective material used to insulate windows. This is available in auto supply and hardware stores. It acts similarly to Mylar, and you can see through some types, as well.

 Wipes
front-surfaced mirror
stiff cardboard
wood strips
tripod

Wiping one image away with another is the device of sliding one scene off the screen sideways and replacing it with a new scene. A common example of this kind of transition is the wipe from the scene of one character talking on the phone to the image of the person he's talking to. While optical wipes done in a lab can be expensive, you can do an inexpensive wipe right in the camera using a front-surfaced mirror that you slide along a track you've put down on cardboard.

To make the track, tape down two rows of wood strips (popsicle sticks work fine) to a square of stiff cardboard. The rows should be just wide enough apart to hold the edge of the front-surfaced mirror snugly. Punch a hole in the cardboard and fit it over the tripod mount. Then screw the camera onto the tripod over the cardboard and the track is mounted and ready.

Set up the mirror-wipe shot with one scene in front of and one
scene to the side of the camera. The front-surfaced mirror
is mounted at a 45-degree angle in front of the camera.

Set up your first scene in front of the camera and your
second scene off to the side at a 90-degree angle. Keep both
scenes the same distance from the camera to avoid having
to refocus as you change scenes.

To produce the wipe, film the scene in front of you.
When you want to make the transition to the second scene,
signal the actors off to the side to begin, and slide the mirror
in front of the camera along the track. The action to the
side will now replace the scene that's happening in front of
the camera. One note: The mirror will reverse the image
off to the side, so take care not to include signs or lettering
or any other clue that will give the trick away.

If you want both scenes to go on at the same time,
creating a split-screen image, slide the mirror only halfway
across the camera's field of view. Then have both scenes
continue on together.

The two individual scenes: The girl is writing the boy a
letter, which he receives in the next scene.

The final result of the mirror wipe, as one picture wipes the other way. You could also leave the first scene and bring in the second, creating a split-screen effect. Then you can have both actions continue simultaneously. Note that the girl's image is now reversed because she's appearing in the mirror.

 Mosaics
front-surfaced mirror
black masking or electrical tape
a photograph or artwork with titles

A mosaic effect is one in which, as the film rolls, small parts of the picture are revealed one by one until the picture is complete, or, starting with a complete picture, are blacked out until the picture is black.

To create such an effect in your film, place pieces of black tape on a front-surfaced mirror, using any shapes you want, regular or irregular. Just cover the mirror completely. Have the mirror set up so that you can photograph a picture, or artwork with a title on it. Shoot several frames with the camera pointed at the tape-covered mirror. Remove one piece of tape, and shoot several more frames. Continue removing a piece of tape and shooting several frames until you've revealed the whole picture.

Ending one scene in a mosaic and starting the next with a revealing mosaic can make an effective transition to another time or place.

 Six-Headed People and Other Kaleidoscopic Images
two rectangular front-surfaced mirrors
adhesive tape
cardboard
protractor
a photograph or other subject

You can make a six-headed image or other kaleidoscopic shots by arranging two rectangular front-surfaced mirrors like this.

Lay the mirrors front surface down side by side on a soft cloth. Measure the thickness of the mirrors, and when you've spaced them their own thickness apart, put adhesive or masking tape across the back of the mirrors to hold them together.

Arrange pieces of cardboard into a V shape, and place the mirrors with the front surfaces facing each other in the V. Make the angle of the V at exactly 30, 45, or 60 degrees to produce symmetrical (the same on each side) images and the proper number of images. Use a protractor to

This image has seven heads instead of six because the angles were a little off. But aren't seven heads better than six anyway?

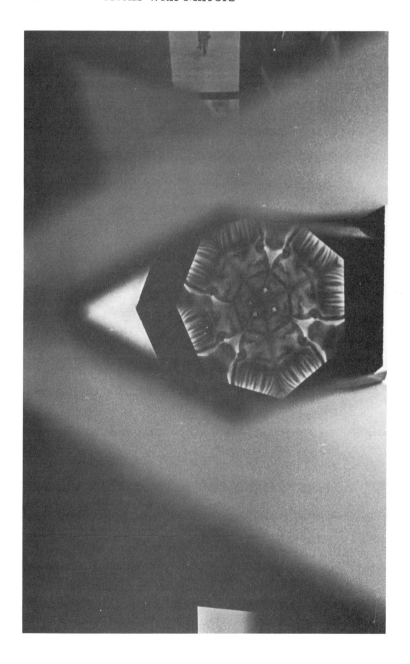

measure the angle, and use tape between the mirror and cardboard for any small adjustments in the angle.

At one end of the V place a small photograph. At the other end, place your camera tilted down toward the mirrors. Be careful not to scratch the lens with the mirrors by mistake. A close-up, macro, or diopter lens will make the kaleidoscopic image larger.

You can try the kaleidoscopic image with live people and outdoors, but you may have more difficulty creating a symmetrical image.

■□■ Putting a Ghost in Your Pictures
beamsplitter
black upholsterer's cloth
dimmer (optional)
cardboard
clay

Your film characters enter a haunted house. They blow talcum-powder dust off the covered furniture. They hear a noise. Terrified, they freeze. Looking at an old chair, they see a ghost materialize right in the chair.

Ghosts appearing in your films or photos can really startle an audience as well as your characters. So can other things that look or act like ghosts. You can photograph a ghostly cat or dog, dress your friends like aliens, angels, or leprechauns, or shoot ghostly baseball caps or doughnuts suspended from threads. Whether for dramatic or comedic effect, ghostly images can add an extraordinary touch to your still photos and films.

There are two basic ways to create ghosts. One method is superimposition, which requires backwinding your film to double expose it. You'll have to either backwind a few seconds of movie film by hand, have a camera that backwinds, or use a separate backwinder. (Ask your camera dealer. They run about $30.) For still photos, you'll need a camera that you can adjust so that you can double expose a frame. (See under Double Exposures and Superimpositions in Chapter 7.)

The other method to create ghosts requires using a beamsplitter (called a partially silvered mirror and available for less than $10 from the Edmund Scientific Company, Edscorp Bldg., Barrington, N.J. 08007). A beamsplitter will give you a sharper image and will be easier to control.

To create a ghostly effect by superimposition, first get a shot of an empty chair at half the correct exposure (that is, underexpose one full stop). Then backwind the film and reshoot, again at half the correct exposure, but having your ghost walk in and sit in the chair. The chair will appear in full exposure, but because your ghost is only half exposed, he will appear, well, ghostly.

Set up your scene in front of the camera and your ghost off to one side. The beamsplitter placed in front of the camera will marry the two images into a ghostly effect.

You can try double exposures with actors, but they will have to freeze their position while the ghost enters. Otherwise they will appear to have double images and give the trick away. You can get around this by having only your ghost in the picture when it appears, and then cutting to a separate reaction shot of your actors. If you want to put the ghost and other live characters in the same shot, the easiest method is to use a beamsplitter.

Mount a 3-inch-by-4-inch beamsplitter at a 45-degree angle on a piece of strong cardboard. Modeling clay makes a fairly sturdy mounting surface. Punch a hole in the cardboard so that you can position it between the camera and a tripod mount with one edge of the beamsplitter nearly touching the camera lens. The rest of the beamsplitter should cover the camera's field of view.

Have your actors set up in front of the camera. Your ghost-to-be should be off to the side at a 90-degree angle to the camera. Lighting needs to be equal for both the front and side scenes, so shooting indoors is recommended for the best control of the lighting. Keep the background of the ghost dark, using black upholstery cloth as a backdrop if necessary.

With a camera that views through the lens, you can line up your actors and an empty chair in front, and ask your ghost on the right to walk forward and sit on a box or chair covered with black cloth that's the same height as the chair in front. What you'll see through the lens with the beamsplitter in place is the ghost walk into frame and appear to sit down in the chair. If your camera doesn't view through the lens, correct for parallax (see under Parallax in Chapter 2), but try several shots to ensure that in at least one of the shots the ghost and chair line up correctly.

Ghost? What ghost? You must be kidding. How'd he get into the picture?

For an even more dramatic entrance of the ghost, still with the beamsplitter method, set the ghost's light on a dimmer switch you can buy for a couple of dollars in a hardware store. Your ghost can already be in the darkness sitting on the cloth-covered box. Bring up the dimmer switch, and the ghost will materialize, already seated in the chair. To de-materialize the ghost, dim the lights out. Without a dimmer, to have your ghost disappear, simply have him walk out of the frame off to the side of the camera.

SEVEN

TRICKS WITH
TIME AND MOTION

Not surprisingly, the essence of motion pictures is motion. People and things can zip into, out of, and all around in your movies. You can move your camera toward or away from action, and even turn it upside down to produce some startling effects. Movies can also distort a sense of real time, too. Ever wonder how a movie could tell someone's whole life story in less than two hours?

Tricks with time and motion can let you compress or expand time, make people appear to fly or to climb the side of a building, or make real people act like cartoon characters. Learning the techniques of playing around with time and motion can enable you to add these and other tricks to your films.

Making Someone or Something Appear or Disappear

The space raider reaches for the alien. Poof! The alien is gone. The pirate looks for a treasure. He closes his eyes,

Another case of now you see them, now you don't. You can make people or objects pop on screen or off at will.

and miraculously, the treasure appears out of nowhere. Making someone or something appear or disappear can startle or amuse an audience.

One way to make someone appear is this. Start filming the scene. At the moment of appearance, have your actors freeze and the new character walk to where you want him while you continue filming. Now have the other characters react and finish the scene. When you edit the film, simply cut out the section where the character walked in.

To have someone disappear, again have the other actors freeze while you continue filming and your disappearing character walks out of frame. Then let the action continue to the end of the scene. Later, cut out the section of the character walking out of the frame. This method gives you the most control over keeping the camera in the same position.

If you want to edit in the camera, you can yell, "Freeze," have your actors stop and also stop filming, then have the character walk in or out of frame, yell, "Action," and start filming again. The only problem with this method is that sometimes you jar the camera when you start and stop filming, and some cameras give you two or three flashed frames whenever you start or stop filming. These flash frames might have to be cut out later anyway to make the scene look continuous.

Whichever method you use, making someone pop onto or off the screen can be a lot of fun to film and a lot of fun to watch in your movies.

Reversing the Action

When people do something backward in your films, it can look funny, unusual, or just plain weird. Even more startling is to see people jump from pools up onto diving boards, or

Nothing to cry over with this spilt milk. We're going to make it pour itself back into the original glass.

milk pouring itself from a glass back into the carton above it, or someone's Halloween makeup put itself back into jars.

One way to make people do something backward in your films is simply to have your actors do whatever it is backward. Even walking backward is hard to do realistically, though. The results will probably look a little phony and not be very convincing.

Some projectors will project a scene in reverse. This would be one way to handle the reverse pouring or diving trick. Your projector may not reverse, though, or you may prefer to have your backward scene as part of a whole movie without interrupting the flow of the film to play with the projector. If so, use the following technique.

Have the action go forward as usual, but film the action with the camera upside down. When you edit the film, flip it over so the end of the scene is now the beginning. Also flop the film from one side to the other so the sprockets are in the right position for projection. When you project, the scene will appear slightly out of focus, but the action you filmed will now appear backward on screen. You can correct the focus on the projector during the screening.

Filming upside down and backward is a good way to stage a safe accident. Instead of having a bicyclist crash into someone walking, start with the two touching and have them back up a step. Film this upside down. When you flop the film, it will appear as though the two were colliding. Now cut to a shot where both are already on the ground, and you've created a real-looking accident without doing harm to the bike, the rider, or the pedestrian.

If you want to preserve the left-to-right look when you flop the film, shoot the upside-down scene through a mirror.

For another method of making people and things go backward, see under Optical Refilming Tricks (Backward Action) in Chapter 8. That method has the advantage of keeping the backward-action scene in focus.

◀▌ ▐▌ Speeding Up the Action

Showing people, or anything else, moving faster than normal, like in the old-time movies, can be done fairly simply with the right equipment. One way is to shoot at the speed of silent film (18 frames per second) and project the film back at the faster speed of sound film (24 frames per second). If you have access to one of the projectors that has its own fast-motion setting, you can shoot at normal speed and simply set the projector to speed up the action. Another way is to use one of the advanced cameras that has adjustable speeds. In that case you could film at slower than normal speed, called undercranking. When projected back at normal speed, the actions appear faster. Light has less time to strike the film when you shoot at slower speeds, so check the owner's manual to see if the camera adjusts automatically for less light, or if you will have to make a manual adjustment of the speed.

You can also speed up actions by shooting a few frames of film, stop filming for a few seconds, shoot a few more frames, stop filming, and so on. When the film is projected, the cars and people will appear to jump around the screen at highly accelerated rates. Even with the camera on a tripod, though, you may jar the camera starting and stopping and give away the trick. You may also have to edit out flash frames that some cameras create whenever they start and stop.

The most controlled way to speed up actions is to single-frame with the camera on a tripod and the single-framing done with a remote control switch that doesn't jar the camera. Some sophisticated cameras come with a built-in timer, called an intervalometer, which automatically clicks off a frame of film at a given interval that you can set. The results of single-framing by remote control or an intervalometer can produce rolling clouds and their shadows that scurry

This silent camera single-frames pictures. The remote
control (from a different manufacturer—it was cheaper)
lets you single-frame without jarring the camera. This
camera also has an automatic intervalometer, which lets you
single-frame at preset intervals of time.

rapidly and dramatically across a landscape, cars that start
and stop and start again at an intersection at super speeds,
traffic lights that blink on and off at a dizzying pace, and
so on.

Speeding up actions that normally take hours or days,
called time-lapse photography, effectively compresses time
in your film. Set up your camera in a spot where it won't be
disturbed. Using either an intervalometer or a separate timer
that will trip the shutter a frame at a time, you can make a
morning glory appear to open in seconds, show all the traffic
in your kitchen for several days in a few minutes, or shorten
the week-long, floor-to-ceiling redecorating of a room in

your house to a matter of minutes. Using a camera with an automatic exposure meter will take care of lighting differences at different times of the day. Plan ahead, because your camera will be tied up for as long as the event you're filming takes in real time. The super-fast results, though, will be worth your patience.

Creating Slow Motion

Two lovers see each other across an open field of flowers and in slow motion run, seemingly forever, toward each other. A drop of water slowly tumbles toward the ground and with elegant beauty spatters in a dramatic pattern. An egg rolls off a table oh so slowly, the audience holding its breath as it approaches the ground.

One way to create slow motion with actors is to have them try actions such as running or walking in slow motion. The effect is a little unreal, but might work for a few seconds or be played for laughs.

For objects or people moving in real time, slowing down the actions can be done with a camera that can film at speeds faster than normal. You would film a glass of milk pouring, for instance, at a speed faster than the normal 18 frames per second for silent cameras or 24 frames per second for sound cameras. When projected at normal speed, the milk will float lazily out of the glass. Remember, though, that when you film at faster than normal speeds, light doesn't have as long to strike the film. Check your owner's manual to see if your camera compensates automatically by letting in more light, or whether you have to adjust the camera manually to let in more light.

If you don't have a camera that overcranks (films faster than normal), you might have a projector that will project fewer frames of film per second, giving the appearance of slow motion. This technique, though, usually makes the action look very jumpy. One other way to create slow motion is by refilming with a rear screen projector. That technique is explained under Optical Refilming Tricks (Slowdowns) in Chapter 8.

▇▇ Animating Models, Titles, and More

Models   You can make clay characters appear to grow and and move, toothpicks and golf balls march across a table, or whole little model towns bustle with activity by using single-framing techniques.

Easier for many than drawing or cutting out cartoon characters, animating models or objects lets you create whole stories and personalities from everyday objects you find around your home. Mirrors can become lakes, sand can be used for shores, and posters or photos can become landscapes in the background. Clay is especially fun to work with, because you can make objects and characters appear to grow and bend. You can even make the clay figures change facial expressions.

Choose a tabletop or flat surface to set up your objects or model town. See how large a field of vision your camera has, that is, how far from side to side on the surface and how far from front to back the camera will hold focus. All the action will, of course, have to take place within that field of vision if you want it in focus.

Have the surface near a large window, or set up enough indoor lights for filming. With the camera on a tripod, if possible, use a remote control switch to film a frame or two at a time. Some cameras allow you to close down the viewing system so no light flares through the back of the camera; this enables you to film without having to sight through the camera for each frame, thereby reducing the chances of jarring the camera as you view.

Objects can move into frame smoothly by shooting several

frames of emptiness, then a frame or two with the objects moving slowly into frame. Now move the objects into slightly different positions. Shoot a few more frames, move the objects again, and so on. To time the swiftness of movements, remember that 18 frames of silent film make up one second of action in your film.

You can shoot objects in apparent real time, or start adding other tricks. You can make objects appear or disappear simply by adding or removing them between filming. The objects will appear to pop onto or off the screen. You can also move the camera sideways or up and down, change focus, or even zoom in or out. Just move the camera or lens a little bit between shootings. The result will look like a smooth pan, tilt, or zoom.

You can orchestrate many objects moving at once by changing the position of lots of objects between shootings. You can even add music later, making the objects appear to dance or march to a specific beat.

Animating models and other objects in this way can take a long time. It may take you many minutes of moving objects around and filming to produce just a few seconds on screen.

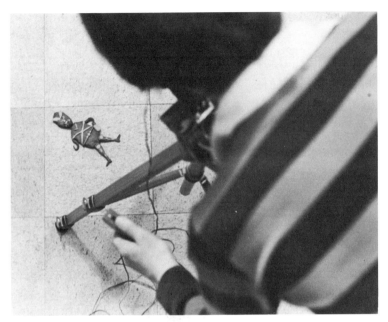

The clay man as he will appear in his final few single frames. Note the use of the remote control switch in the photographer's left hand.

The way the clay man will appear on screen is first a head, then a head and body with arms, then a head, body with arms, and also legs. If you build a clay man first, you can start with him whole and have him come apart in pieces by single-framing, too.

So be patient. You can have a lot of fun creating this kind of imaginary, magical footage, and your results will be well worth the time and effort.

Animating Titles, and Other Ideas You can also animate titles for your films. Take a drawing or photo and place it flat on a table. Cover this with a sheet of clear acetate onto which you'll rub letters. (Both clear acetate and lettering

You can single-frame letters one at a time to spell out titles for your films.

are available from art supply stores, which are listed in the yellow pages of your phone book.) Using single-framing techniques, you can add the letters one at a time every few frames and they'll appear to pop onto the screen and spell out words.

To make full words appear to unwrite themselves, spell out the words first, and remove a letter at a time while you single-frame. The words will appear to unspell themselves.

You can animate handwriting by single-framing a little bit more of a signature or word on each frame. You can even make maps and show how the troops move through the jungle from village to village in your films. Single-frame a red solid or dotted line, adding a portion of the line every few frames, until the whole shot is completed.

◾ Animating People (Pixilation)

Animating objects and models is fun because you can control what they do. But you can even animate people (called pixilation), making them do crazy things almost like cartoon characters.

Have some friends sit on the ground, feet and hands out in front of themselves as if they were driving a car. With the camera on a tripod, click several single frames. Now have your friends move forward a few inches, and pose in the same position. Click a few more frames.

You may have to pan the camera slightly each time you single-frame, and your friends may get a little tired of shuffling along on the ground, but wait till you see what you've filmed. Your friends will look like they're puttering around by motor power. Add a few sound effects, and the result is uncanny.

Pixilation looks a little crazy and is lots of fun. You can do this with people in any position, or even design a whole film, complete with costumes, around the device. Races are

particularly good, whether you have your actors look like they're driving or riding horses, bikes, or motorcycles (without the actual props; just add the appropriate sound effects later). Anything from head-on collisions to winning by inches looks hilarious on screen with this technique.

Double Exposures and Superimpositions

Want to give your character a sad face and a happy face at the same time? You can do it by giving him two heads with a double exposure, that is, shooting two shots on the same piece of film.

To double expose still pictures, you need to shoot one picture and then *not* advance the film. Simple box cameras are great for this, as you normally have to roll the film ahead. Instead, simply leave the film in place. More sophisticated cameras have devices that prevent you from double exposing by mistake. To double expose on purpose, you have to find a way to get around such devices. Read your owner's manual or check with a camera store to find out how.

To give someone two heads, shoot the first shot with the person's head to one side. With his body in the same posi-

Rev 'em up and they're ready to go. Animate people like cartoon characters by single-framing them moved a little bit at a time.

tion, and the camera locked in place, have the person shift his head and change expressions. Without advancing the film, shoot again. If the background is very dark, you can shoot both shots at full exposure. For a less than dark background, shoot each shot at half the correct exposure (one stop underexposed). The result, because there are two shots on one piece of film, will look correctly exposed. A dark or black background has the advantage of avoiding a possible shift of the camera between shots, which would create a double image of the background in the picture.

You can double expose two completely different images, too. Or you can make it appear that two things are beginning at the same time. If you want a face or some object to appear clearly, though, try to compose the second shot so the face from the first will appear in the second shot against something dark.

You can also triple expose or quadruple expose pictures. Follow the same steps for double exposures, but use a third or a quarter the exposure setting for each shot.

In movies, a double exposure is called a superimposition. A super is often used to indicate who or what a character is thinking about.

To achieve such an effect, show the person in one shot, and superimpose the image of another person or place onto the first one. You need to be able to backwind the film to the point you want to start the superimposition, then continue filming the new shot. The same rule of halving the exposure for double exposed still shots applies here also.

Double exposures or supers can add a very beautiful or artistic effect to your stills or films. Careful planning for what you want in both shots before you shoot will help ensure successful double exposures and supers.

 Fly Like Superman
　　　　　a raised flat surface
　　　　　an electric fan (optional)

You will believe a boy or girl can fly. And look, Ma, no strings.

Have your first shot of your character going into his leap. The third shot will be him appearing to land.

The shot in between, the one of the character flying, is done by placing the character flat on his back. You can use a wagon with a board over it, a table, a bench, or a car top, and shoot from a low angle. Have the character extend his arms, lift his legs off the surface, and keep his head level or with his chin tilted toward his body. Film with the camera upside down. Have the character appear in the bottom of the frame as you see it, with nothing but blue sky above him. Make sure there are no references such as trees in the sky.

When you cut this shot in between the other two, flip flop it as described under Reversing the Action earlier in this chapter. Your character will now appear to be flying, with nothing but blue sky below him as he looks ahead or down on the world below. The shot will appear slightly out of focus. If you don't want that, see under Optical Refilming

It's a bird, it's a plane, it's . . . your friends flying in your own films!

Tricks (Backward Action) in Chapter 8, on refilming with a rear screen projector.

If you want a little extra realism, use a fan to blow your character's hair around, and add whooshing sound effects. This is one piece of film magic your friends will go crazy trying to figure out how you did it.

Climbing Up Buildings
      a board painted to resemble the wall in your first scene
      a black cloth or other neutral background

Your character is trapped against the side of a building. There's no escape. Suddenly, he turns around and starts climbing right up the side of the building. The bad guys are foiled again.

To do this trick, select a building with a smooth wall that you can match in color with a painted board. Shoot so you don't see any background that has up and down references, such as trees or telephone poles.

Shoot the first shot of your character appearing to start climbing the side of the building.

Cut now to a second shot. Have your character on the board you've painted to match the wall. You can have the board on the ground, in which case set the camera horizontally. For an even more realistic look, set the board at a 45-degree angle, and also the camera at that same angle. Make sure the background has no trees or similar references, as they would appear horizontal or at an angle. A neutral background

The grunting and goaning is more and more real as our spidery friend appears to climb the side of a building. The black background (from a fabric store) hides the trees so as not to give the trick away.

is best. If you haven't shown a background in the first shot, you won't have to worry about matching backgrounds.

After you cut in the shot of your character climbing the tilted board, cut to a shot of the character entering a window or peering out a window on an upper floor. Your audience will believe he really did climb the side of that building.

The Six Million Dollar Man Effect

A six million dollar man effect is one where the character in your film miraculously leaps up to the top of a wall, car, or other object. The trick involves editing several shots together. Have an adult help you with this trick, especially in selecting a safe object for the actor to jump from. A jump onto even a low object will be astounding to your audience, and this safe way is the only way this trick is intended to be done.

Your character wants to leap up to the top of a wall four feet high, a feat no ordinary human could do. First shoot the character approaching the wall. Pan with him as he runs, crouches, and leaps up. In the film, you'll cut this shot right after he leaves the ground.

The second shot is the real heart of this trick. Set your actor on the wall. He's going to jump off the low wall backward, which will give anyone a funny feeling. But he's going to have to do the jump with his hands up and his head looking up, not down; that is, the position he'd be in if he were jumping up. That may make your actor feel even funnier. Another good reason for a short leap. Shoot the actor's jump down with the camera upside down, and for even greater effect, from a low angle. When you edit this shot

This running approach, jump, and landing all look real, even though the actor actually jumps down. Make sure you have an adult with you when you shoot this trick, and pick a low object to appear to jump onto. It will still look terrific.

into the sequence of shots, you'll flip flop the film as described under Reversing the Action earlier in this chapter. The shot will be slightly out of focus, but it will look like the character is jumping up. In the film, cut off both ends of this shot, the parts where the actor is already on the wall and where he lands on the ground.

For the third shot, have the actor jump up and down on top of the wall as though he were just landing. Edit into your film only the part where he comes down, and the landing will look natural.

The fourth shot would be the character running out of frame, as though he leaps onto high walls every day and there's nothing unusual about it.

If you wish the second shot in this sequence to be in focus, see the section under Optical Refilming Tricks (Backward Action) in Chapter 8 for how to achieve the effect by refilming.

To make the jump seem longer, you could film it in slow motion, or you could cut in an extra shot of a close-up of the character as he jumps. Adding sound effects later will help accentuate the jump, and also help distract your audience from how it's done.

Have fun with this trick, but take care to do it safely.

EIGHT
REAR SCREEN PROJECTION AND MATTE BOXES

Optical tricks—from simple dissolves, to binocular effects, to complicated split-screen shots—are usually done in a laboratory by an optical printer. Opticals can be costly, though, and there are ways you can produce similar versions of the same effects for very little money The techniques described here use a rear screen projector and a matte box, both of which you can build yourself.

Some of the tricks involve refilming footage you've already shot. Other tricks require passing film through the camera twice. Still others are based on backwinding of the film. Whatever the extra effort involved, though, homemade opticals give you an opportunity to add some professional-looking pizzazz to your pictures.

Building a Rear Screen Projector
cardboard box
flat black spray paint
X-acto knife or razor
front-surfaced mirror
tracing paper or rear screen projection material

Building a rear screen projector is not difficult at all. The first step is to paint the inside of a cardboard box with flat black spray paint. The box must be at least 2 feet wide by 3 feet long by 2 feet high. Cut a rectangular hole toward the bottom left of one of the vertical sides. This is the hole through which light from a movie or slide projector will enter the box. The light will hit a front-surfaced mirror you will later place at the corner of the box on the inside, positioned to the side with the first hole at a 45-degree angle. At the spot where the light reflected from the mirror will strike the adjacent, long side of the box, cut a slightly larger rectangle. If you've purchased rear screen projection material (available from Edmund Scientific Company, Edscorp Bldg., Barrington, N.J. 08007), cut the hole so the material will fit snugly into it. If you plan to use tracing paper, the size of the hole is less critical. Spray paint the outside of the side of the box where the light will emerge after striking

A rear screen projector is inexpensive and easy to build and will enable you to do a number of different optical tricks.

the mirror. Tape tracing paper over the hole, preferably on the outside of the box.

That's the whole rear screen projector. The purpose of the box is to control the image that you're refilming. The mirror allows you to refilm without aiming the camera directly into light from a movie or slide projector. The flat black paint on the inside and the one outer side help eliminate any light that may flare into your camera as you refilm. The textured surface of tracing paper or rear screen projection materials spreads the light evenly so hotspots don't ruin the pictures.

Backwinding Techniques

A few expensive cameras have a built-in backwinding system. You just run the film, put the lens cap back on, cover the back of the viewing system, backwind the film to whatever point you want, then shoot again. Simpler cameras do not have such features. You can buy a separate backwinder for around $30 from a camera store. Or, if you want to backwind for just a few seconds worth of film, though, without investing in more equipment, you can try this method. Open your movie camera. Place a piece of masking tape over the pin that takes up the film into the cartridge after it's exposed. Now film the scene you want. In a dark place, such as a closet or changing bag, open the camera up again. With your finger, push the film you've exposed back into the feed portion of the cartridge. Three pushes would equal one second of film, and you can only do this for about 5 seconds worth. Remove the masking tape from the take-up pin, close the camera, and film the second scene. Because the film was not firmly taken up the first time through, you've photographed it for a few seconds, producing your effect. It's easier to do backwinding by hand toward the beginning of a roll of film, because the take-up portion of the cartridge is mostly empty.

When you use this backwinding technique, you may not have completely accurate registration of your film, and you may lose the footage setting on your camera (most cameras reset each time you open the camera). So you'll be doing a little guesswork this way, but you may get perfectly adequate results.

Optical Refilming Tricks

You can produce a number of effects on a scene you've already shot by refilming, and in some way or other modifying, that first footage. Some of those effects are fades, dissolves, superimpositions, speedups, slowdowns, backward motion, freeze frames and blowups.

Set up in the movie projector the film you've already shot. Arrange the projector, the rear screen projection box, and the camera so that the image of the scene to be shot exactly fills the camera's viewing area, that is, make sure you don't include in your second scene a rough black border around the first. Your automatic exposure meter will let you know if you have enough light. If you have too much light, place a neutral-density filter in front of the lens.

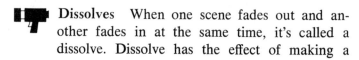

Fades Fades can be done in the camera, as described previously. But if you're not sure where you want to fade a scene, shoot it normally first then produce the fade where you want it in the scene during refilming with the rear screen projector.

Dissolves When one scene fades out and another fades in at the same time, it's called a dissolve. Dissolve has the effect of making a slow transition from one time or place to another. A long dissolve might be appropriate for a romantic film. Shorter dissolves will give a slow, easy pace to any film when you want to avoid the abruptness of a direct cut to the next scene.

To produce a dissolve, film one scene with a fade-out, in the camera. (This is the scene that you'll project into the rear screen projector.) On a new roll of film, shoot the fade-in, but at half the correct exposure (one stop under). Rewind this film in the camera and now set up your camera to refilm with the rear screen projector. Project the first fade-out, refilming it over the new fade-in at half the correct exposure (one stop under). When this second roll is developed, you'll have a dissolve between the two scenes.

 Superimpositions Supers, as described under Double Exposures and Superimpositions in Chapter 7, are two scenes that are filmed one over the other.

To produce a super, film the first scene normally, or use footage you've already filmed as the first scene to project into the rear screen projector. Film the second scene on a different roll at half the normal exposure (one stop under), then backwind the roll. Now, while the first scene is being projected into the rear screen projector, refilm it over the second scene, again at half the correct exposure. The result will be a correctly exposed superimposition.

The advantage of using the rear screen projector is that you can control how much to superimpose, and also you don't have to shoot both scenes back to back, which is sometimes impractical or impossible depending on what the two scenes are.

Speedups Use a projector that can speed up action. Refilm at normal speed, and the new scene will now be speeded up permanently.

Slowdowns   Use a projector that has a slow-motion setting. Refilm at normal speed, and the new scene will now lazily appear that way always.

Backward Action   Project in reverse a scene that was filmed normally, and refilm it onto a new roll of film. The scene will be backward now.

This use of the rear screen projector eliminates the need to film upside down and flip flop the film when you want to reverse the action. The new reverse-action footage will also be correctly focused, and can be cut into your movies without having to refocus the projector during a screening.

Freeze Frames   Freeze frames are those dramatic opticals, often at the end of a film, where the action simply stops and the last picture remains frozen on the screen.

You can use a movie projector that has a still-frame setting. Refilm the scene to the point you want to stop and keep filming while the projector freezes on that one frame. Note that most projectors have a screen that comes between the film and the bulb so the film won't burn up. That will reduce the amount of light, so expect the frozen image to be a little darker.

Another method to produce a freeze frame is to have the frame of a scene you want frozen made into a slide. Check with your photo store or in the yellow pages to locate a laboratory that will do this. Use a slide projector, then, to project this slide and film the slide for as long as you want the freeze. You can even fade out at the end if you like. Now cut this new footage into your film after the original scene and you'll have a closer match in terms of lighting intensity.

Blowups   You can refilm, or reshoot, just a portion of a scene or slide on the rear screen projector. In effect, by adjusting the image size as you project, you can eliminate portions of the picture you don't want. When you refilm, the result is a blowup version of the original.

When you refilm footage, do expect the new footage to be a little grainier than the original. You may also have some strobing problems, which means that the projector and the camera doing the refilming may not record everything frame for frame. The camera might record the dark flickers between pictures, as well as the pictures themselves.

One way to reduce the possibility of strobing is to shoot the original footage at silent speed, 18 frames per seconds, and do your refilming at sound speed, 24 frames per second, and if possible, with a low-light camera. The faster speed will help eliminate some of the flickering you are apt to get if you film and refilm at the same speed. Also, if your projector has a variable shutter opening, set it at the wide angle. You'll have to plan to project and shoot the rest of the roll of film at sound speed with this technique.

If your projector has various speeds, experiment a bit. Mark the settings you choose with a piece of tape and keep notes on which setting was used for which several feet of footage. One of the speeds will most likely produce reshot footage with no strobing.

Live-Action and Still Titles
rear screen projector
rub-on lettering
tracing paper or a pane of glass

With a rear screen projector, add titles to live-action footage. Shoot a scene and project it into the rear screen projector.

The ragged edges cut into the rear screen projector will be
eliminated when the footage is framed properly in the
camera. The titles can be added over either a slide or a
movie scene.

Put rub-on lettering on glass, or directly onto the tracing
paper if you're using that for a screen. Now refilm the live-
action scene with the titles. This way you can have titles
over pans of the ocean, moving shots from a car window,
or whatever the first or last scene of your film might be. You
can also project a slide or freeze frame of a filmed shot into
the rear screen projector and film titles over this still
picture. If you use lettering on glass, double check your
depth of field so that both the projected scene and the lettering are in focus.

Monster Movies
rear screen projector
flexible model of a monster

You can make a model monster or dinosaur attack or threaten a character in your film. Film the scene with your character, keeping him to one side of the screen. Project this footage into the rear screen projector, setting up your model in front of the rear screen. Light the model to the same intensity of your footage. Keep the model's lights from spilling onto the rear screen. Advancing the footage with the projector's inching knob one frame at a time, refilm the scene. Move the monster a little for each frame and refilm with a remote control switch, like in animation, one frame at a time. Your monster can appear very big compared with your character. You will need a small aperture to get as large a depth of field as you can so both the footage on the screen and the monster remain in focus.

 Binocular and Other Shapes
rear screen projector
black construction paper

Binocular effects are fun when your character is looking through binoculars in one shot, and then you cut to whatever the character sees. To produce the shape of binoculars around a shot, film the scene first. Then project this footage into the rear screen projector. As you refilm, have someone hold a piece of black construction paper with a binoculars shape cut out in it in front of the rear screen image.

With a slide, you can even create the appearance of moving binoculars. Have your character in the first shot look through his binoculars, moving his head sideways. Then in the refilmed shot, project a slide into the rear screen projector. As you refilm, have someone move the black binoculars cutout in the same direction the character has moved his head, and have the camera pan along with the movement of the cutout. When you cut this into your film, your audience will get the sensation of binoculars scanning across a scene.

You can cut out other shapes in black paper in addition to the binocular shape. Cut out heart, cross, or star shapes to showcase a still or moving picture. You can produce a wipe, eliminating a scene altogether, by drawing black cardboard across the image until the refilmed scene is all black.

For an even classier fade or wipeout, use two pieces of black cardboard and close off the scene by sliding the two pieces together from the sides until the image goes all black. Then open the next scene by starting the refilming from black with the two pieces of black cardboard already in place. Now slide each piece aside, making the refilmed image appear from the center out until it fills the screen.

Building a Matte Box
soft plastic container
flat black paint
X-acto knife or single-edge razor blade
plastic slide mounts
cardboard
stapler or masking tape

You can build a matte box for movie and still cameras. Spray flat black paint on the inside and outside of a soft plastic container and its lid. The tubs used for ice cream, margarine, and other foods are just right for this. A still camera will require a deeper container; flatter containers are better for movie cameras.

When the paint has dried, cut a rectangle out of the lid that is the size and shape of a plastic slide mount (available at photo stores). Staple or secure with masking tape two strips of cardboard to the outside of the lid, above and below this rectangular hole so that a slide mount will slide snugly into and fit between the cardboard and the lid. The piece of cardboard, in whatever shape you choose, that you insert into the slide mount is called the matte.

Cut a round hole in the bottom of the container itself large enough for the container to fit over your camera lens. If the fit is not completely snug, use black tape or even black cloth strips to make the fit both snug and light tight.

You can purchase matte boxes that attach to your camera's lens from a photo dealer, but they can cost $30 and up. With a little patience and skill, you can build your own matte box for pennies.

This homemade matte box is set up to do an up and down (vertical) split screen effect. You can cut cardboard to irregular shapes, too, and slide them into the slide holder.

This commercial matte box, complete with adjustable bellows, is set up to produce a heart-shaped vignette.

 Split Screen Effects
matte box
small piece of black cardboard
plastic slide holder

With movie cameras, use the matte box to create two different scenes going on in your movies at the same time. Cut a piece of black cardboard that will fit into the plastic slide holder, covering half the image area. Place the slide in the lid of the matte box. Film the first scene you want. Now backwind the film as described earlier in this chapter. Switch the black cardboard so it is now covering the other half of image area. Film your second scene. When developed and projected, the two scenes will appear to take place side by side.

You could also produce this split screen effect on a rear screen projector. Shoot one scene with the action on one side of the frame and project this into the rear screen projector. As you project, cover the half of the rear screen image that will not appear in the final version. Refilm and then backwind. Now thread up a second scene you've shot where the important material appears on the other side of the image area. With black cardboard, cover the other side of the rear screen image as this footage is projected, and refilm.

Having One Person Walk Into a Tree and Lots of People Walk Out
matte box
tall, vertical object
black cardboard

A funny effect is to have one person walk into a tree (or car, phone booth, phone pole, or other unlikely object) and lots of people parade out on the other side. This trick is a specific application of the split screen effect.

Use a matte box and choose an object that has a fairly regular or straight up and down line. Make a matte to match this line and, while the matte blacks out the rest of the picture, film your character walking into or behind the tree or object.

Now make a matte for the other side of the image, called a countermatte. Backwind the camera, as described earlier in this chapter. Film again, this time having lots of people parade seemingly out of the tree. Even if you use something as thin as a sign pole, your actors can just walk through the scene without worrying about being seen on the wrong side of the screen and giving away the trick. The countermatte is blocking them out on the side of the screen where the one character was in the first pass of the film through the camera.

The finished result will make it look as if not just one person but a whole crowd of people have been able to conceal themselves behind or inside an object only a few inches wide.

■□■ **Multiple Image Effects**
matte box or rear screen projector
black cardboard

Seeing more than one image on the screen at the same time can be exciting in both stills and movies. Different actions can seem to happen at the same time, you can comment on one image by showing another simultaneously, or you can create a sense of beauty, pattern, and movement by having more than one image strike a response in an audience.

For stills, you can use a piece of black cardboard in the matte box to cover half the image area. Shoot the shot and, as in a double exposure (described under Double Exposures and Superimpositions in Chapter 7), don't advance the film. Shoot at the proper exposure, however. Now reverse the cardboard and expose the other half of the shot. This is a still version of the split screen.

You could also create this effect by projecting a slide or movie frame into the rear screen projector so that the part you want to include fills just half the image area. Use black cardboard to cover the remaining half of the rear screen material. Rephotograph with your still camera, but don't advance the film. Now project a different image onto the other side of the rear screen and cover the unused part with the black cardboard. Snap the shutter again, double exposing that frame of still film. When developed, the result will be a still, multiple image.

Instead of having a person walking into a tree, you can turn a car and its driver into a motorcyclist zipping by. Matte out along the pole line on one side, backwind, and then matte out the other side. You can even let more than one vehicle come out of the pole, making the car appear to turn into lots of motorcycles, cars, vans, buses, and more.

With the matte box or rear screen projector, you can create mattes of different shapes that will block out less regularly shaped areas than just half the image area. You could make mattes to cover one quarter, half, then three quarters of the image area to produce four pictures. Or mattes that would make three diagonal stripes, each holding a different picture.

Multiple Images with Front Screen Projection
two or more slide or movie projectors
projection screen or white cardboard
rub-on lettering (optional)
pane of glass or piece of acetate (optional)

Bombarding audiences with images, or just placing two or three images side by side, can add whole new and different meanings to the images from when they are viewed separately. One way to create such multiple images is called front screen projection.

Set up as many slide or movie projectors as you like. Project images onto a projection screen or bright white cardboard. For still shots of a movie frame, use a projector that can stop on one frame. With a still camera, and as close to the line of projection as possible, rephotograph the images. You can also refilm already shot footage, a series of changing slides, or both slides and movies into new multiple-image footage. Always keep the camera, whether movie or still, as close to the line of projection as possible. (Please refer to the information on strobing in the section on Optical Refilming Tricks.)

If you want, you can also overlap images you're projecting, creating instant double or triple exposures.

You can even add titles to slides or movies with front screen projection. Place lettering on glass or acetate and

Using front screen projection you can combine titles with
a slide or movie screen.

reshoot the slides or scenes with the lettering between the
camera and the screen. Make sure you have enough depth of
field to hold both the lettering and pictures in focus.

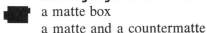 ### Changing a Scene's Background
a matte box
a matte and a countermatte

Using a matte box, you can change the background of your
scene if you don't like it, or it doesn't fit the movie you're
shooting. You could add mountains to a scene that originally
didn't have mountains in the background, for instance.

Shoot your first shot with a piece of cardboard cut to the shape of whatever you want to include in the scene. Slip this cardboard into the lid of the matte box. You may have to experiment a little to get the shape just the way you want it, especially if the area you want to change is irregularly shaped. After the first shot, backwind the film. Place a piece of cardboard with the exact opposite shape of what you've just shot in the matte box. That piece is called the counter-matte. Now reshoot, replacing whatever was first cut out of the shot with the new image. When developed, the original action will now be combined with a new background, creating an entirely new image, and perhaps feeling, to the scene.

NOTE: It is often difficult to get good registration, even with a commercial matte box. Try several times, if you can, to help ensure that one of the shots will come out.

With still cameras, you can create the same effect. Just shoot with a matte, don't advance the film, and then double expose at full exposure with a countermatte.

Vignette Effects
a matte box
mattes

You can use the matte box to create shapes to focus your audience's attention on an image. You can use star, binocular, cross, heart, or simply circular or irregular shapes to confine, accent, or showcase your pictures. Unlike the sharp lines you can create with these cutout shapes on a rear screen projector (see Binocular and Other Effects, earlier in this chapter), when shooting through such shapes on a matte box, the shape line will be much softer, creating the vignette (pronounced veenyet).

This round vignette strongly accents the subject in the center of the picture, in this case a statue of Captain Hancock, a famous Los Angeles figure.

NINE

AND MORE TRICKS

Some tricks don't quite fit into the categories as defined in this book. And some tricks, which are neat to do in films, like scars or burns, are technically makeup, rather than camera, tricks. These have been included in this section, so that you can get just as tricky in front of the camera as behind.

Combination Tricks

Combination tricks are those that require using two or more of the tricks mentioned earlier in the book to create one effect. For instance, you can shoot a mosaic effect, but through textured glass, for a whole new effect.

Or, you can use the Six Million Dollar Man effect, but with a model plane instead of a person, superimposing an explosion at the end of the shot.

Combination tricks can be as unlimited as your imagination. Use the tricks simultaneously or in sequence to create the kind of effect you want for your stills and movies.

This combination trick adds to a vignette of the statue, a double exposure of the flowers. Both shots were done at half the correct exposure (one stop under), and the black background on the vignette helped create a good overall exposure.

Blood, Sweat, Tears, Scars, Bruises, and Burns

While not technically camera tricks, adding makeup tricks, which put all the gore of blood and guts into your films and stills makes them more realistic and more fun to do. Here are some simple ways to produce the following effects.

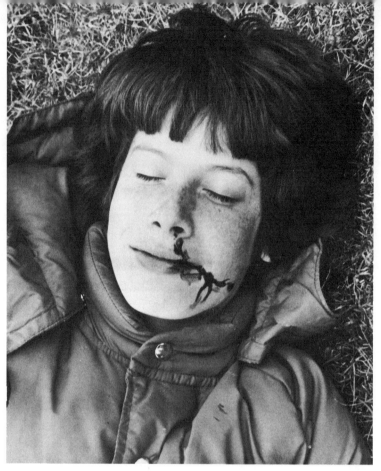

Chocolate syrup makes great blood for black and white films, plus you can eat the makeup afterward.

Blood
chocolate syrup (for black and white)
a straw or Q-tip
corn syrup (for color)
red food coloring (for color)

For black and white film, chocolate syrup makes great blood. Apply with a plastic drinking straw or Q-tip. The best part is that you can eat the effect after shooting. For color film, use clear corn syrup mixed with red food coloring for another edible effect.

Sweat
household sprayer
corn syrup

When your character is supposed to look all worked up, but doesn't want to run around the block one more time, spritz him with water mixed with a little clear corn syrup. Use a household sprayer filled with the mixture. The result will bead up and glisten like sweat. This one requires a good face washing and perhaps a shampoo afterward. And don't forget to rinse out the sprayer carefully, too.

Tears
corn syrup
straw or Q-tip

Clear corn syrup straight from the bottle applied *carefully* with a plastic drinking straw or Q-tip below an eye will bring a tear to your character and your audiences. Have plenty of tissues for all.

Scars and Bruises
surgical adhesive
powder
Q-tip
rouge or lipstick
eye shadow

Over stretched skin, put surgical adhesive (the kind your mom might use to put on false eyelashes). Hold the skin stretched until the adhesive is dry. When it's dry, release the

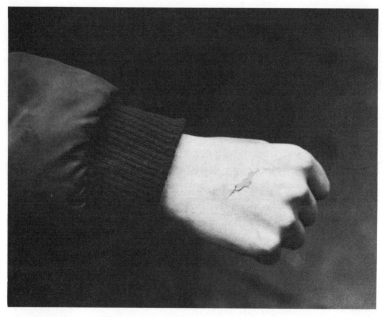

An ugly scar like this is easy to make with a little surgical adhesive (available at cosmetic counters).

skin, letting it snap back, and rub the area slightly. A ridge of scar tissue will appear.

For bruises, use several layers of surgical adhesive, letting each layer dry over stretched skin. Powder each layer lightly with a powder puff after it dries. Let the skin snap back after three or four layers. With a Q-tip, add a bit of lipstick or rouge to turn the area into anything from a scrape to a cold sore. Add a little green, blue, or purple (plum) eye shadow to turn the area into a glaring bruise.

> **Burns**
> spirit gum
> cotton ball
> a coloring material

Dab a little spirit gum (available at drug stores or from your local high school theater or drama department) on the flesh. Plop on a cotton ball and pull away from the skin. The remaining cotton can be colored with anything from rouge to shoe polish to give your characters the look of anything from a rosy burn to a full roasting.

◾ Lightning, Explosions, and Smoke

You can create lightning by scratching the emulsion side (the dull side) of your movie film with a pin. Make a jagged line like lightning seem to grow a little bit on each frame, carefully making sure the lightning is positioned in the same

When you film in tight on the model house, it will look like it's smoking on the top.

spot on each frame. When projected, the white projector light will make the lightning appear to streak across the sky. You can also add a few flash frames of clear film to give the impression of great flashes of white light instead.

Real explosions in films have to be done by experts. A safe way to do explosions in your films is to trick your audience this way. On darkened film, scratch the emulsion side in a pattern of dots or shot lines. The first frame would be a center ball scratched out. The next frame would have a few dots radiating from the center. Each subsequent frame would have more dots or lines coming farther out from the center, while the center ball dimishes as the explosion takes place. The explosion lasts for only a few seconds, and lets you seem to blow up your models without really harming them. You can also try explosions on clear film, making dots or short lines with black or colored marking pens.

You can make smoke rise out the chimney of a model house (or wrecked model cars or trains), by putting a little flour on the end of a straw or flexible clear plastic tubing such as the kind used in fish tanks. Puff a little air through the tube, and a puff of smoke will appear.

APPENDIX

MORE PHOTO BASICS

Some basics appy to both still photography and movie making. These include composition, exposure, depth of field, lighting, and how to keep the camera steady.

Composition

You may have heard it said about an artist or photographer that "she has a good eye." That means the person knows how to frame a picture to include just the objects needed. It means the person has balanced color, large and small objects, lines, spaces, and even textures (the surface quality) of objects to make a pleasing, effective picture. Someone who has "a good eye" knows how to compose a picture well.

Many people have a natural talent for composition. It is also, however, a design skill that can be learned. The best way to learn more about good composition is to study as many photographs as you can. Old *Life* and *Look* magazines in the library contain many examples of professional photographs. You will find many good examples of composition, although you may think of an even better way a photo might have been composed. Composition has no right or wrong way; the judgment depends entirely on the taste of the photographer and the viewer of the photograph.

Here are a few tips that will help you make better photos.

1. Be very careful of what's in the background in your photographs. Are trees or power lines growing out of your subject's head? An uncluttered background makes it easier for your viewers to understand what you're trying to say or show in your photograph.

2. Off-center balancing means not dividing your picture into exact halves. If you film the ocean, try not to put the lines of the horizon right in the center of the picture. If you're taking a photo of a building, try not to have it smack in the center of the picture. Generally, pictures are more interesting if the main object is slightly off center, and other objects in the picture are balanced around the main object.

3. Frame your central object from time to time with other objects that appear naturally in the scene. This creates a sense of depth as opposed to flatness. It also may help to tie the elements of the photo together in a more pleasing way.

4. Keep your photos simple.

A still photographer can choose to shoot his subject horizontally (across) or vertically (up and down) within a rectangular format such as that of a 35 mm camera. He can even have the picture cropped (trimmed) in the darkroom later on. Cropping would remove unwanted or unnecessary parts of the picture so a viewer could concentrate on the main subject.

Filmmakers are limited to the horizontal format in their photography. Parts of a scene can be blown up to eliminate unnecessary elements, but unless you do this yourself, which is explained under Optical Refilming Tricks (Blowups), it can be costly.

To make yourself aware of better composition in your pictures, (1) think through what you want to say on film and arrange the elements in the picture to make that statement, (2) shoot a scene more than once and in more than one way if necessary, (3) study your results, seeing what you did for the compositions you do like, and (4) *practice* taking pictures and filming.

Types of Film

Understanding how to use film properly will help you not just in getting good results when you try the tricks in this book, but in your regular photography as well.

Film is a strip of plastic (the base) that has been coated with light-sensitive chemicals (the emulsion). Many film stocks have sprocket holes on one or both edges of the film so sprockets (gears) can pull the film through the camera. Most films are made to be developed in light-tight conditions outside the camera. Instant cameras use film that contains chemicals capable of developing in daylight within minutes after exposure.

The two major types of film are black and white film and color film. In still photography, black and white has always remained the cheaper medium to work in, and has never lost its popularity, even to the more spectacular looks of color film. Black and white film allows the photographer a great deal of room to explore moods, and is actually better for many subjects in terms of creating a reaction in an audience.

Color film is the standard today for movies. It's now very difficult for amateurs to even find black and white movie film, or get it developed, and it's actually more expensive than color. If you get the chance to run some black and white through your movie camera, you may find it adds a special look or mood you're just not used to seeing in color.

Films are also divided into negative films and positive (reversal) films. The standard for black and white still film is negative film. The negative is exposed, and in a darkroom, this negative is developed, then blown up on an enlarger onto positive paper, which in turn is chemically developed. Black and white film can also be turned into slides, though this is rarely done today. Black and white movie film can be either positive or negative. If the original that's run through the camera is negative, a positive image is struck for viewing and editing. Then the negative is "conformed," meaning matched scene for scene, to the edited positive (called a work print) to make release prints.

Negative film is the standard for producing color prints. The suffix "color," as in Kodacolor, always signals negative color film. Reversal film is the standard for producing color slides. The suffix "chrome," as in Fujichrome or Ektachrome, always signals reversal color film. You can make slides from negatives or prints from slides, but you increase your costs and may lose some quality in the transfer.

In movies, negative 35 mm is the movie industry standard. Like black and white, a positive is struck and edited, and later the negative is conformed to the positive work print to produce more positive prints for release to the public. Super-8 uses positive color films such as Kodachrome and Ektachrome as its standard stocks. If you wish to preserve this camera original from scratches, you can have a duplicate struck and work with that for editing. Then the edited version can be used to conform the "camera original," a better term in this case than "negative." Release prints can then be struck from this conformed camera original.

Editing Tricks

The element of surprise is what makes trick photography so exciting. In order to create surprise in your films, you have to know what the audience is expecting to see, and then show them something totally unexpected. While there are many tricks you can do with your camera, there are some magical things you can do with editing.

Editing tricks break into two categories: tricks based on staging your action and camera position, and tricks based on the order in which you choose to arrange the pieces of film. In this section, we'll look at one method of staging your action for surprise—reverse angles—and three methods of arranging the pieces of film—smooth cuts (any kind of editing that cuts in and out of a scene without calling attention to itself), jump cuts (the opposite of smooth cuts), and altering time.

When you've found the frame you want to cut on, stop running the film through the editing machine (or viewer) and mark the frame of film with a light-colored grease pencil.

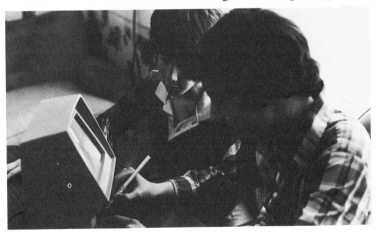

This piece of film is about to be cut on the splicer. Another cut piece will then be spliced to this first piece with a tape splice made specially for Super-8 film.

Smooth Cutting   Making a smooth cut from one shot to the next requires—

1. Changing the image size.
2. Changing the camera angle.
3. Cutting on a movement, color, or shape.

To cut on a color or shape means to match the screen position of the object in the last frame of shot 1 to the one in the first frame of shot 2. Cutting on a movement means not only matching the screen position of the object (which in this case is a moving object) in shots 1 and 2, but also the direction of the movement.

To accomplish a smooth cut, a technique called overlap and matching action is used. An example would be the filming of an actor sitting down on a bench. In shot 1, the actor sits down and is filmed in a medium shot. In shot 2, the actor sits down again and is filmed in close-up. This fulfills the requirement that the image size be different for a smooth cut. To fulfill the second requirement, we would also change the angle at which the camera films him in the second shot. The editor can now cut from shot 1 to shot 2, matching the action of the actor at any point where the audience's eye will go to the same screen position. The movement has also been planned to go in the same direction in both shots.

What's the advantage of a smooth cut? For one thing, you can save or otherwise alter screen time. If it takes 10 seconds in real time for an actor to approach a bench, sit on it, and get comfortable, you can shave this to 3 seconds of film time by making a smooth cut. Second, smooth cuts keep the flow of the film going. In a trick that you don't want the audience to notice, you might want to plan for a smooth cut into and out of the trick.

Ignoring the Rules for Effect To make a different statement with editing, you can take all the rules just mentioned and completely ignore them for effect. If you change the image size from shot 1 to shot 2, but not the camera angle, you produce a pop cut, which is very disturbing. If you overlap and match action, but cut a few frames previous to the point where screen positions match, you create a curious effect called the reverse phi effect. In the case of the actor sitting on the bench, he would appear to start sitting in shot 1, then for a moment appear to have been lifted backward, then continue to sit. Also a very disturbing effect.

To create excitement in an audience, you may choose to avoid smooth cutting and edit a number of shots with what's called jump cutting. In jump cutting, you plan *not* to match shapes. For example, the object at the end of shot 1 is on the left. The object at the beginning of shot 2 is on the right. The audience has to move their eyes to keep up with the action, a trick that without their realizing it, excites them.

Reverse Angles   Smooth cutting, especially of dialogue scenes, often involves what are called reverse angles (or over-the-shoulder shots). In shot 1, we see Alice over Bill's shoulder. In shot 2 (the reverse-angle shot), we see Bill over Alice's shoulder. Shot 3 in the scene might be a close shot of Bill's face (with no over-the-shoulder). To go from shot 1 to shot 2, though, notice that Bill always stays on the

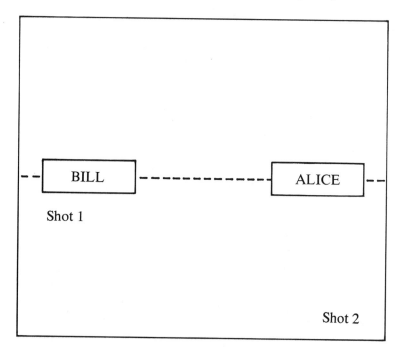

left of the screen and Alice on the right. The audience stays with the scene and is not confused.

To accomplish reverse angles, look at the floor plan for shooting. The dotted line, called the stage axis, is an imaginary line between the actors. Whichever side of the line the camera is placed on for shot 1, as long as the camera stays on the same side of the stage axis, the characters will always appear on the same side of the screen, in this case Bill on the left and Alice on the right. Notice where the camera was placed to produce shots 1 and 2.

If you were to cross the stage axis while the camera was moving, or if the actors moved in front of the camera, you would not confuse the audience because they would see exactly what was happening. If however, you crossed the stage axis while the camera was off, and then began shooting, the reverse-angle shot would move Alice and Bill to different sides of the screen with no explanation. The result may be audience confusion. If the effect you want is to disturb your audience, go ahead and break the rules by crossing the stage axis without alerting the audience. They will have the feeling something is wrong, but will not know quite what.

Other Ways to Alter Time   While overlapping and matching action can shave some time on screen (reduce real time), you can also use a technique called cutting in and cutting away for the same purpose. The scene might be set up this way:

1. Establishing shot
2. Medium shot
3. Close-up
4. Cut in to an extreme close-up
5. Cut away to another character or object
6. Reestablishing shot

Playing dialogue or other sounds over the cutaway, and making the cut a smooth one, will disguise the fact that you've altered real time.

Intercutting two stories, or using parallel action in scenes of different types or styles, is another technique to alter time. When you want to indicate that two actions are happening at the same time, you use intercutting, that is, you actually show first one action, then the other, then go back to the first, then back to the second, and so on. But the audience understands and accepts that the actions are supposed to be simultaneous.

Optical Effects: By Editing or in the Camera?   A number of optical effects, such as fades and dissolves, can also be done in the editing process, though many of them, as described earlier in this book, can be done in the camera as well, and usually at quite a bit less expense. The best approach is not to limit yourself to either kind but decide on one or the other according to which will achieve the most control and the best possible effects in your filmmaking and storytelling.

Filmmaking Tips

By using different image sizes, camera movement, graphics, and sound, you can add immensely to your storytelling bag of tricks.

Image Size   Image size refers to how big an object looks on screen. A long shot might show a character and the background. The character appears fairly small in the frame. Long shots are often used to establish where you are in a scene or story. A medium shot brings us closer to the object or character, cutting out most of the background, which could be a distraction if the character or object is doing something important you want the audience to see. A close-up makes the object or character, or a part of the object or character, appear very large on the screen, essentially eliminating everything else from our view. The audience is forced to concentrate on what the character or object is doing or saying, because the filmmaker has chosen to give them nothing else to look at that might distract them. Close-ups are very important in capturing reactions, which are a way of letting the audience know how a character feels about whatever action is taking place in the story.

Camera Movement   Panning, tilting, tracking, dollying, and booming all refer to different ways a camera can be moved during filming, and each has its own particular effect.

Rotating the camera horizontally while filming is called panning. To get a smooth pan, point one foot in the direction in which the pan will end and hold it there. Then start the pan from the beginning and continue it through to the end without a break. The simple foot technique will keep you from jerking your body at the last moment to get the end of the pan and the result will be a smooth horizontal shot.

Tilting is simply panning up or down, rather than horizontally. Again, the camera remains in one spot, though what the camera sees is extended by its movement.

Tracking is moving the camera horizontally with the action. Professionals use elaborate carts and tracks to make these shots smooth and seemingly effortless. You can put the cameraman in a shopping cart, hand cart, or on a skateboard. Shooting from the window of a moving car can also be an effective tracking technique.

A dolly shot is like a tracking shot, but instead of going with the motion of the action horizontally, the dolly moves either toward or away from the action. A dolly shot is different from a zoom shot in that a zoom shot never changes its perspective. It simply brings the picture closer or makes it recede into the distance without ever leaving the spot from which the picture is photographed. With a dolly shot, on the other hand, the camera physically moves through space.

To see the difference, look at something across the room with your fingers making a rectangle. Now make the rectangle smaller and focus on an object. That's what a zoom does. To simulate a dolly shot, hold your hand in the original rectangle. Now leave the rectangle the same size and actually move across the room. See how objects now pass in front of, alongside, and then behind you. When the object fills as much of the rectangle as it did in the "zoom" shot, you've finished. But you can see the effect of moving through space is quite different. Sometimes a zoom is the only way to do a shot, say, of a boat across a lake. On the other hand, if you put us on a second boat and dollied in on the first, the scene would have a whole different feel to it.

Boom shots are when the whole camera is moved up or down. Again, perspective changes. On professional films, expensive cranes and booms are used to raise and lower the camera. You might be able to make boom shots simply by raising or lowering your whole body. For more spectacular shots, you may have a building in your city with an elevator on the outside. Riding a forklift or piece of farm machinery may also give you the same results, but take extreme caution and always have an adult with you for such adventurous endeavors.

Graphics   Graphics is a term that refers to the combining of composition and movement to make a dynamic picture. For example, a car driving across a desert in a long shot has less impact on an audience than a shot of a rocket going up. Why? Horizontal movement is less dynamic than vertical movement. But what if the car is passing across a roadside full of trees, and you're panning along with the car. Now you have a kind of strobing effect, and there is a great feeling of movement and excitement. Having characters or objects move diagonally across a screen, or viewed from underneath or overhead if that's not the usual viewing angle, can create dynamic graphics that keep an audience interested. The shot of a front door opening rarely causes a stir. Shoot the door from a second-story window, and what appears on the screen is unusual. It may even at first disorient your audience until they catch on to what you are doing. You can use graphics to aid in your tricks, though like all techniques, they will be most effective when they fit the story and are not used just for the sake of using them.

Sound   While slide shows can contain sounds, creating reality with films can be especially enhanced by the addition of sound. You don't have to shoot sound that's synchronous (happening at the same time) with the picture. Sounds can be shot wild (at a different time) and added to the film after it's edited. So you don't need a sound camera to make movies with sound. A cassette recorder may be all you need.

The major categories of sound are dialogue (people speaking), music, and sound effects. Most sound tracks are a blend of all three. With one cassette recorder, you may have to record first a dialogue passage, then music, then effects in sequence. If you can borrow another recorder to mix sounds, or play a record in the background while characters talk or do some action, you can combine all three in the recording. You may be able to control your sound track better if you can record dialogue, music, and sound effects separately and mix them together after the film is edited. That, of course, would be more expensive, and sometimes more time consuming. Some hard-to-get sound effects are available on records. Check your library and record stores.

Getting Materials for Your Tricks: Mail Order and Photo Stores

Many of the materials mentioned in this book are available from around your home or can be purchased in camera stores, art supply houses, or hardware stores. Check the yellow pages of your phone book for local suppliers. Some items are available more cheaply and readily through mail order. You can write to these companies for their catalogues:

Edmund Scientific Company
Edscorp Building
Barrington, New Jersey 08007

Porter's Photographic Equipment & Supplies
411 Viking Road
Cedar Falls, Iowa 50613

Many photographic magazines have ads for other companies that provide photo supplies and services. If you do order by mail, be patient and plan ahead. It may take several weeks to get the item your ordered.

Films can be processed through local film, drug, or discount stores. Many companies also process film through mail order. Be sure to follow the instructions carefully if you do send film through the mail, paying particular attention to the amount of postage and including your return address with the payment. Some companies, among them Kodak, provide prepaid mailers.

When going out to buy your supplies, just entering the photo store can sometimes be bewildering. The bigger stores have different sections for cameras, darkroom equipment, lights, and so on. Even smaller stores may make you feel a little uneasy, especially if you're not exactly sure what you're looking for.

Camera stores and the people who work in them, though, can make your trick photography efforts much easier. They may have just the right kind of filter or recommend just the right book for you. Make friends with one of the more experienced salespersons, and you'll not only learn a lot, but you'll have someone to get advice from when problems crop up.

Check with your photo dealer and discount store for prices on film as well as other photo equipment before buying. And look into used equipment, too, to get the most for your money.

Some Recommended Reading

You will find many books on photography, some of which contain material on trick photography, in your library, book store, or photo store. There are also a number of excellent magazines available at the same locations. Libraries often have back issues of these magazines, or try obtaining them from the publisher or used book and magazine stores.

Your school or public library is a storehouse of information on photography. Just ask, and librarians will be pleased to help you find the material you need. Many high schools have photography classes or clubs. These can be a great source of information and sometimes equipment. Both the teachers and many of the students will be highly skilled, and often very willing to help you accomplish the tricks you want to do in your films and still photos. Get acquainted with them, or if you are already in high school, consider taking some of the classes or joining the club.

Pamphlets

The Kodak publications are highly recommended. Available in many photo stores, these guides (most are paperbacks), are well-written, easy to read, and chock full of gorgeous color photographs and illustrations. Examples are the *Here's How* series and *Filters and Lens Attachments*.

Magazines

Magazines such as *Popular Photography, Modern Photography,* and *Petersen's Photographic Magazine* will keep you excited about the possibilities of photography. Every so often, these magazines have articles about trick photography and special effects techniques.

Super-8 Filmaker magazine is a superb blend of information, mostly for the beginner or amateur, but sometimes even for professional filmmakers who use Super-8. There is a column on effects, and often special articles and tips from readers on how to create effects. Many of the filmmaking tricks can be applied to still photography, too. Highly recommended.

Books

Brodbeck, Emil E. *Movie and Videotape Special Effects.* New York: Amphoto, 1968. Quite technical, but has especially large section of matte and models (miniature) photography.

Fielding, Raymond. *The Technique of Special Effects Cinematography.* New York: Hastings House Publishers, 1972. Quite advanced, but a classic in its field. Gives you a good idea just how complex professional trick photography can be.

Hedgecoe, John. *The Photographer's Handbook.* New York: Alfred A. Knopf, 1977. A complete look at photography. Often explains why tricks work in addition to just how they're done. Superb illustrations and many color photographs.

Horvath, Allan. *How to Create Photographic Special Effects.* Tuscon, Ariz.: H. P. Books, 1979. Often technical, but beautifully illustrated with many color photographs of the effects.

Jacobs, Lou, Jr. *You and Your Camera.* New York: Lothrop, Lee & Shepard Company, 1971. Easy-to-understand photo basics. Highly recommended.

Matzkin, Myron A. *The Super 8 Filmmaker's Handbook.* London and New York: Focal Press, 1976. Thorough information on moviemaking. Good mix of photos and illustrations to help you understand the material.

Sherman, Roger M., and Barry Schonhaut. *Simply Super 8: A Basic Guide to Moviemaking.* Boston: Little, Brown & Company, 1977. Good, solid basic filming information written especially for the beginner.

ACKNOWLEDGMENTS

The author would like to thank the following people for their aid with the photographs for this book: Roy B. Radow; Mike, Peppi, Jeff, Andy, and Robby Stern; Patrick de Catalogne; Tina Carey; Mary Ellen Wheeling; Ralph Chojnacki; Chris Murray; Stephen De Guire; Scott Crosby; and Jim Cooper. Thanks also to Schaeffer Photo and Camera Supply, Inc., 6520 Sunset Boulevard, Hollywood, California 90028, for their generous supply of photo equipment.

Many thanks also to my family and other friends for their encouragement and support. Special thanks to camera operator Doug Knapp for his technical expertise and to senior editor Fred Graver for his infinite patience and kind advice.

146

INDEX

147